SEEING GOD
EVERYWHERE

SEEING GOD
EVERYWHERE

A PRACTICAL GUIDE
TO SPIRITUAL LIVING

SWAMI SHRADDHANANDA

EDITED BY
PRAVRAJIKA VRAJAPRANA

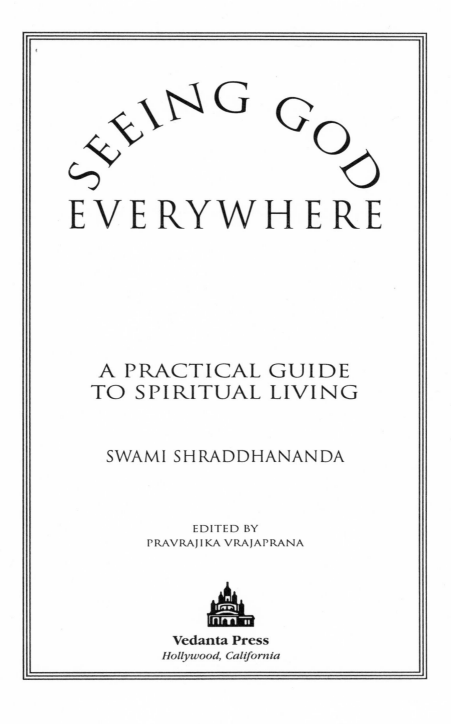

Vedanta Press
Hollywood, California

Vedanta Press
1946 Vedanta Place
Hollywood, California 90068-3996

If you wish to learn in greater detail about the teachings contained in this book, write to the
Secretary, Vedanta Society,
1946 Vedanta Place
Hollywood, CA 90068-3996
e-mail: info @ vedanta.org

Printed in the United States of America.

Library of Congress Cataloging-in-Publication Data

Shraddhananda, Swami, 1907-1996
Seeing God Everywhere: A Practical Guide to Spiritual Living /
Swami Shraddhananda; edited by Pravrajika Vrajaprana
     p.   cm.
     Includes index.
     ISBN 0-87481-052-3 (alk. paper)
     1. Spiritual life—Hinduism. 2. Hinduism—Doctrines.
     I. Vrajaprana, Pravrajika, 1952-   . II. Title.
     BL 1237.36.S49   1996
     294.5'44—dc20   96-9304
                               CIP

Cover photograph copyright © 1996 by James T. Aeby

PREFACE

The genesis of *Seeing God Everywhere: A Practical Guide to Spiritual Living* was an unexpected phone call from Swami Shraddhananda, requesting that a book be created from his writings. (The request was particularly surprising coming from him. A man of great self-effacement, he had summarily dismissed all earlier suggestions that his uniquely inspiring writings be made available to a larger reading audience.) When he was assured that such a project would be considered an honor, he warned with a hint of glee in his voice, "It is a *stupendous* task!"

The adjective was correct in more ways than one. First, as a prolific writer, Swami Shraddhananda had a stupendous body of written material, scattered over three continents in a variety of publications.

But the material in these articles is "stupendous" in the larger sense: Swami Shraddhananda's writings are illuminating and ennobling. The joy of mystical experience emerges from these articles; they assure us that seeing God everywhere is possible; they tell us that one day we *shall* have this experience. In a very practical way, we are shown how we can begin to make this experience a reality in our own lives.

The "stupendous" task was achieved through the help of many people whose unselfish labor brought this book into existence. Many thanks to Amala Kenny for her many hours of typing and for her helpful suggestions. Endless gratitude is owed to Anne Lowenkopf whose editorial ability is second to none, and who was always cheerfully and generously available for consultation. Thanks are also due to Audrey von Bieberstein whose awesome close reading skills were put to the test. Pravrajika Anandaprana was a consistent source of help and support from the book's inception to the last page of the last proof sheet. Enthusiastic from the beginning, her careful reading and judicious advice were invaluable.

Swami Swahananda was a great source of help and support, as well as Swami Sarvadevananda who kindly helped in

vi   locating even the most obscure references. Shelly Lowenkopf volunteered his expertise to provide the book's fine index; many thanks are owed to him. Jim Aeby formatted the book and created the beautiful cover; more than that, Jim was, as always, a joy to work with and his creative input gave the book the quality it deserves.

Special thanks are due to Lalita Maly for allowing us to use her "Instructions to a Disciple" letter which adds so much to the Spiritual Guidance section. We would like to express our gratitude to the Advaita Ashrama in Calcutta for their permission to reprint Swami Shraddhananda's articles which appeared in *Prabuddha Bharata.* We would similarly like to thank the Ramakrishna Math in Madras for their permission to reprint from *The Vedanta Kesari;* to the Ramakrishna Mission Ashrama in Narendrapur to reprint from *Sri Ramakrishna Dipika;* to the Ramakrishna Vedanta Centre in England to reprint from *Vedanta for East and West,* and to the Ramakrishna Mission Ashrama in Kanpur to reprint from the *Banga Bharati Souvenir.* Their kindness and cooperation has been invaluable.

Finally, we are all grateful to Swami Shraddhananda for having written these articles in the first place. All of us who have worked on the book have felt that it was truly a blessing to do so. We are happy to be able to offer this blessing in tangible form to the world at large.

Swami Shraddhananda played a unique role in the Vedanta movement in the West. "You must be able to get into the minds of Americans," he would say, "in order to serve them." And in order to do that, he added, one must be completely familiar with American culture, history, and language. The swami's interest in the Civil War, and Abraham Lincoln in particular, was noteworthy. Lincoln, in fact, was one of Swami Shraddhananda's greatest interests. He referred to Lincoln as "one of my spiritual heroes—*Rajarshi* [King of Sages] Abraham Lincoln." A genuine expert on the subject, the swami amassed over the years an extensive and impressive Lincoln library.

It might seem unlikely that an avid student of Lincoln should have his origins in Bangladesh. But this small nation, while it was known as East Bengal and still an integral part of India, has provided the Ramakrishna Order with many of its great spiritual personalities.

The future Swami Shraddhananda was born in that lush, verdant land in 1907. Hailing from the village of Shobhana (lit., "beautiful") which is nestled by the Bhadra (lit., "gentle") River, the future swami was born the youngest of four children to a grammar school headmaster and his wife. The young boy had a close relationship with his pious grandmother who lived with the family. The old lady loved to worship her Shiva image and taught her grandson to do the same. When she went away on pilgrimage, the young boy was placed in charge of the worship. It was a duty that suited his temperament, for even as a child he liked to meditate. He was still a boy when one of his school teachers introduced him to the ideas of Sri Ramakrishna and Swami Vivekananda.

It is perhaps difficult for Westerners to understand the powerful spiritual atmosphere that has always pervaded Indian life—even more markedly in earlier generations. Religion and the pursuit of spirituality has never been a Sunday affair in India: it has always been considered the highest goal, humanity's most noble endeavor. The spiritual quest has always drawn the nation's greatest individuals—in our age, Sri Ramakrishna, Swami Vivekananda, and Mahatma Gandhi, to mention but a few. It is therefore not surprising that spiritual interests maintained their hold on the future Swami Shraddhananda as he grew older. While he was a teenager, he organized a study group which both discussed the teachings of Sri Ramakrishna and Swami Vivekananda and sang devotional songs. This was an indication of not only his philosophical bent, but also his great love and appreciation for music which remained a lifelong enthusiasm.

The young boy was endowed with a studious nature and a scientific bent of mind. He excelled in school and eventually left his home for Calcutta in order to further his studies. This proved to be a fateful move since it brought him to the Calcutta Students' Home where he came in close contact with the monks of the Ramakrishna Order.

From 1925 to 1937, the future Swami Shraddhananda spent most of his years in the Calcutta Students' Home: first, as a student and resident; later, as a monk and worker. In 1925 the young student received his spiritual initiation from Swami Shivananda (Mahapurush Maharaj, lit., "great soul"), a direct disciple of Sri Ramakrishna and the second president of the Ramakrishna Order.

While at the Calcutta Students' Home, Swami Shraddhananda came under the influence of Swami Nirvedananda, the founder of the Calcutta Students' Home, and as Swami Shraddhananda later wrote, "a very dear disciple of Swami Brahmanandaji [the first president of the Ramakrishna Order]." Swami Nirvedananda's effect on the young student was profound, and they remained in close contact until Swami Shraddhananda left for the West in 1957. "Swami Nirvedananda was one of the great heroes of my life," Swami Shraddhananda later wrote. "It was he who in . . . 1927 initiated me into the analysis of the seer and the seen." This *drg-drsya-viveka*, the analysis of the seer and the seen, deeply influenced the young man; the results can be seen in the articles included in this book.

Meanwhile, the young student received his B.S. degree in chemistry and was continuing graduate studies in the same subject. On Buddha Purnima day [the thrice-blessed day in May] in 1930, the young man had gone to Belur Math, the headquarters of the Ramakrishna Math and Mission outside Calcutta. Although he wanted to become a monk, it was assumed that he would do so after he completed his graduate studies. However, on that holy day, some monks were teasing him about whether he would join the Order or not. "When will you join?" they asked. Picking up the gauntlet, the young student replied, "I am joining today itself!" And so he did at the age of twenty-three.

While a novice, the future Swami Shraddhananda lived at Belur Math and had his spiritual training under the close guidance of the great Swami Shivananda.

From 1934 to 1937, after his vows of *brahmacharya* (first monastic vows), the future Swami Shraddhananda was a warden of the Calcutta Students' Home. From there he was sent to Mysore, in the south of India, to join the famed Mysore Study Circle. The Mysore Study Circle was renowned for the caliber of its scholarship, and for that reason the Ramakrishna Order sent its most promising minds to study there. In both Belur Math and Mysore, the young monk studied widely in Eastern and Western philosophy, psychology, and comparative religion. In 1939, he received *sannyasa,* the final vows of renunciation, from Swami Virajananda, who was then president of the Ramakrishna Order.

Swami Shraddhananda served as Swami Virajananda's private secretary for twelve years, and had the opportunity to live for some years with him in the Himalayas. From 1952 through 1956, Swami Shraddhananda was the editor of the *Udbodhan* magazine, a Bengali-language journal of the Ramakrishna Order, where his literary and poetic abilities found creative expression.

In 1957, Swami Shraddhananda was sent to the United States as assistant minister of the Vedanta Society of Northern California in San Francisco, serving under Swami Ashokananda. When the Vedanta Society of Sacramento became independent from the Vedanta Society of Northern California, Swami Shraddhananda became its head. He served in that capacity from its inception in December 1970 until his death in July

X

1996. He passed away just as he had lived—with tranquillity and great peace.

During his long life, Swami Shraddhananda helped many spiritual seekers, not only through his vast correspondence, private interviews, and public lectures, but also through his considerable literary output. He authored many Bengali books and articles. His earlier English book is entitled *Story of an Epoch*, which details the life and work of Swami Virajananda along with the early history of the Ramakrishna Order. Swami Shraddhananda also wrote many articles for various journals in America, India, and Europe. The articles that are included in this book are what is hoped to be the best representation of his work.

In a January 1 1988 letter to a devotee, Swami Shraddhananda wrote: "'May you be illumined,' the Master's [Sri Ramakrishna's] blessing on thirty-five devotees on this day in 1886, was for all devotees of all times." We sincerely hope that this book will give the inspiration to make that blessing a reality.

CONTENTS

CONTENTS

CONTENTS

Part 5
SPIRITUAL GUIDANCE

THE
SEARCH

A Fruitful Search for God

THOSE WHO SEEK GOD ARE often frustrated in various ways; they do not understand whether or not it is possible for their search to be fruitful. Some seekers complain, "I have tried meditation. I have tried concentration and prayer for two years, or three years, or four years, but illumination has not come." Others complain that they have tried to meditate upon God in different ways and are confused about what God really is.

When we are interested in seeking God, we should first settle upon which God we are seeking, because different pictures of God are given in different religions, and even in the same religion different concepts of God are found. Further, the emotional and intellectual constitution of each mind is different; it is only natural that different people will approach God in different ways. If the seeker cannot decide which particular idea of God to meditate upon among the innumerable concepts of the Divine, he or she should seek the guidance of a competent spiritual teacher. If this question is not settled, one's spiritual life is bound to be confused.

Some people like to think of God as an impersonal truth— as infinite Reality, infinite Consciousness, and infinite Bliss. They should stick to this idea of an impersonal God. It may happen that a person whose basic aptitude is for the impersonal God may, after reading devotional literature, develop an interest in meditating upon God with form, such as Christ, Buddha, Shiva or the Divine Mother. This seeker may continue in this way for some time, but eventually may not find joy and peace. The contemplation may not be fruitful.

On the other hand, consider the case of a person who has an emotional nature and wants to love God tangibly, in a personal way. If by reading different philosophical and metaphysical books the seeker tries to meditate upon God as the Infinite Principle, he or she will not find meditation interesting. There will be frustration. Therefore, an important point to

2

decide upon in the very beginning is which aspect of God appeals to me and what God should I seek.

Then another trouble comes: our impatience. We begin with a certain notion of God and continue for some time, and then we become restless. Not finding "instant illumination," we then try another concept of God. Then another. We drift from concept to concept. This drifting is a great hindrance to an effective search for God.

After the *Ishta,* our Chosen Ideal of God, has been decided upon, we should give sufficient time for that contemplation to become effective. Sri Ramakrishna's parable of digging a well in one place is very instructive. If a person digs just ten feet or twenty feet in one spot and, not finding water, gives up and goes on digging again from place to place but nowhere sufficiently deep, he or she is bound to be frustrated. Had this person dug a little more, say thirty feet, water would have been found. Sri Ramakrishna said that impatience often comes in our religious life, and it is a great obstacle. *Ishta-nistha,* clinging faithfully to one's Chosen Ideal, is extremely important.

Sri Ramakrishna began his search by worshipping God as the Divine Mother, with the help of an image of Mother Kali, and in a spirit of absolute self-surrender and burning faith. Sri Ramakrishna was like a child with total faith in his mother, knowing that whatever she did was best for him. With that kind of faith, Sri Ramakrishna pursued his spiritual practice.

But it was not an easy path. We suffer greatly if some worldly desire is not fulfilled, but an earnest spiritual seeker's frustration in not attaining the vision of God is one hundred times more painful. The aspirant has withdrawn his or her mind from many sense enjoyments and has sacrificed many things for God. If God does not respond, an acute suffering overwhelms the aspirant's whole being. This happened to Sri Ramakrishna. He suffered for months because Mother Kali remained like a motionless stone. But he did not give up; his faith sustained him. Then one day a miracle happened: Mother responded. Beyond any doubt Sri Ramakrishna felt that Mother was formless, infinite Consciousness. This vision naturally brought him great peace of mind, but his dependence upon the Mother continued. We can imagine his attitude: "O Mother, I shall always remain your child. You have blessed me with this vision, but I

cannot say that this is final, so I depend upon you. Kindly hold
my hand and take me wherever it is necessary for the perfection of my spiritual life." As a result of this self-surrender, wonderful things happened. The Mother began to give him many
other experiences. To Sri Ramakrishna, all these different
visions of God, personal or impersonal, were just the different
faces of the Divine Mother. At every step his search became
fruitful.

If we have sincerity and patience, our search for God will
be fruitful—no matter with what idea of God we begin the
search. By God's grace, more and more of the truth of God and
our own real nature will be revealed. Two confusions exist in
spiritual life: We do not know who or where God is, and we do
not really know who we are. This ignorance regarding God, ourselves, and our world is called *maya*.[1] A fruitful search for God
enables a person to cross over maya.

When we look at ourselves we seem to be very tiny compared to the vast universe. Wherever we go we are confronted
by the duality of the little and the great. We go to a library and
see thousands of books on the shelves relating to various sub-
jects. How little our knowledge is compared to the storehouse
of knowledge contained in those volumes! A sense of frustration and insignificance overwhelms us. We go on a trip to a
high mountain range and find that we can barely climb a few
thousand feet, while the vast stretch of peaks all around mocks
our littleness. We sit in a restaurant where we are allowed to eat
as much as we like for a certain sum. Having paid the sum we
begin eating, but soon the stomach refuses to accept any more.
Again there is a sense of frustration: "I wish I could eat double
this quantity, but I cannot." This is our experience. And it is
equally true in the areas of love, wealth, happiness, friendship,
honor, and so on. The vast and the little invariably go side by
side. This conflict can be resolved only by spiritual wisdom.

God-consciousness is a discovery on two levels. It is discovering my spiritual nature and discovering God, the Infinite, who
is hidden by the glare of empirical existence. He is hidden by

---

[1] Maya is the cosmic illusion that creates ignorance and veils the vision of
Brahman, the one Reality. Due to the power of maya, Brahman is perceived
as the manifold universe.—Ed.

4   nature, He is hidden by life, by my mind, by all the sense experiences. As I grow spiritually, I discover both God and myself. My physical and psychological nature may be limited, but my spiritual nature is not. I am really Spirit. Spirit is much more than nature, much more than mind, much more than life. In the process of this discovery, my fears and doubts about myself slowly begin to disappear. There cannot be any fear, doubt, or confusion in my true Self. Spiritual progress means progress in the comprehension of my spiritual nature as well as comprehension of the infinite, changeless Reality, God.

Why am I searching for God? Many people seek God when they are in a crisis—whether of health, economic condition, or some other worldly difficulty. If God listens to their prayers, they say, "Oh, God is kind." If their prayers are not answered, they lose faith. On the other hand, if they have true faith, they say, "It is God's will; let His will be done." Their faith is not shaken.

We are on a spiritual search because we are seeking God for peace and strength. We are not satisfied with the world as it is; it is continuously changing. We are not satisfied with this body; it is fast approaching its seventieth year, the deadline in the horoscope! We are afraid, so we want to lift this fear. We are seeking something stable, a knowledge that will bring us the joy of Totality. We are not satisfied with a little knowledge, with little tidbits of pleasure. The saints and sages tell us that one who has realized God becomes free from all evil, passions, fear, pettiness, and ignorance. Even though living in the body, the illumined soul feels this freedom. We read in the Bhagavad Gita that the Self cannot be burnt by fire, killed by weapons, scorched by heat or withered by wind.[2] That Self is our true nature, the principle of pure Consciousness within this transient body.

In a genuine spiritual search, we seek God in order to discover that we really are parts of the infinite, immortal Being. Our true Self shares the nature of God. If we can find God through our search, we shall simultaneously find the Self. We shall find ourselves eternally related to God; our lives will be grounded in that endless love. The fear of death will vanish

---

[2] 2. 23.

forever. When we become conscious of God, we have neither future nor past. We live in an eternal, timeless present. We also rise above the fetters of space. The vast universe can no longer frighten us.

If our purpose is pure, and we seek God for God's sake—that is to say, if we seek God in order to be aware that we are filled with God—we shall certainly be able to discover that God is our own essential truth. Entering the body, God pervades every pore as Consciousness, the Brihadaranyaka Upanishad says.[3]

It is very important to know where to seek God. We often seek God outside, in heaven after death. The great seers and teachers tell us that if we are seriously seeking God, we should try to see His presence first within ourselves. It is He who is enabling us to see, hear, smell, and work. There are people who have had this experience: they always feel that it is God who directs their lives; from this realization self-surrender comes.

In a wonderful hymn to Lord Shiva, Swami Vivekananda describes him as the infinite calm at the back of all the noise of this universe.[4] In another verse he implies that the wild mind, with all its desires and distractions, is, in fact, the dance of Shiva. If we can look upon our wild minds as the dance of Shiva, the wildness of the mind will disappear in two seconds; that is the miraculous touch of God. If we can touch anything with the Divine, it will be transformed at once. So when we seek God, we should search within. If we are able to feel His presence in the movements of our bodies and minds, we shall become purified.

The practice of inner contemplation gradually enables us to see God's glory outside. The tenth chapter of the Bhagavad Gita prescribes the contemplation of God in nature. Wherever there is any manifestation of power or excellence, whether in a mountain or in a tree or in a human being, the Gita teaches us to see the presence of God in that object. This can be another search, the search for God in nature. But it is better that this search be done after we have progressed a little in trying to experience God within ourselves.

[3] 1. 4. 7.

[4] "A Hymn to Shiva," *The Complete Works of Swami Vivekananda,* 8 vols. (Calcutta: Advaita Ashrama, 1976), 4: 501-04.

6

At no time in spiritual life should we give way to depression. There is nothing in spiritual life to be depressed about.

God is simple, and the search is also simple. The main factors necessary in this search are faith, self-surrender, and sincerity. Sri Ramakrishna said that if you take just one step toward God, God will come ten steps toward you. We should retain our faith. We should neither read too much nor should we allow our minds to be scattered in too many directions. Somehow we have been imprisoned in this little life; if we can develop a desire for freedom, our search is bound to be fruitful.

We should remember that spiritual experience is a process. It is not that all of a sudden we find ourselves illumined. Illumination is happening every day. When we sit in contemplation even for fifteen minutes, we should feel that we are in the presence of God. We are repeating His holy name; that is communion, that is an experience of God. If God is the power and the love in ourselves, then how can we miss Him? If the Vedantic definition of God as the Totality is clear, we can find God every day.

As our contemplation grows deeper, the sense of God's presence becomes stronger and stronger. Of course the mind goes outward when we are very busy with our secular activities and involvements, but just as soon as we find some time to close our eyes, we are bound to feel the presence of God. We can hear God's voice saying, "I am with you; I am with you."

We should have a spirit of self-surrender. Let God drive this life. Surely, He is a responsible driver. He is my eternal friend, my eternal companion. As these experiences become clearer and clearer, we will become fearless, strong, and detached. Then we shall walk in this life with freedom; we shall not be afraid of anything—not even of death. Unnecessary desires will not crowd into our minds any more, because we know that by experiencing God we experience everything. We enjoy everything through God. This is the real fruition of spiritual life. A fruitful search for God is indeed possible.

Spiritual life will to bring us to the state in which the small personality disappears and our divine nature appears.

THE WONDER
THAT IS GOD

OF THE MANY PATHS THAT lead to God, wonder should surely take first place. The towering mountain range, the glory of a sunset, the vast ocean, the forests and fertile plains—all these can throw the mind into a mood of wonder. We look at the world of nature and ask: Who could have made this world and guided all of its movements? The answer that comes from within says that there must be an infinite Intelligence at the back of this world because we find that everything behaves according to laws, principles, and design.

The emotion of wonder can prompt our quest for God. A scientist who seeks to resolve nature's mysteries is at an advantage if his or her heart is humble and receptive to the wonder of God, for nature more readily reveals her secrets to those whose love for God has quieted the human ego. Think of the humility of Einstein who, through his scientific research, became convinced of a divine Intelligence. Similarly, Isaac Newton drew a parallel between intellectual knowledge and the vastness of the ocean, declaring that he "had been vouchsafed the privilege of gathering a few pebbles on the shore." Such thoughts should convince us that the more closely one deals with nature, God's wondrous handiwork, the closer one is drawn to the Infinite. The pettiness of the human ego diminishes in direct ratio. The ego is bound by the limits of this universe, but the great unseen Intelligence behind all things visible and invisible is continuously creating inexhaustible wonders.

The world's great scriptures stress the spiritual importance of utilizing the wonder of God for meditative purposes. Sri Ramakrishna used to relate the anecdote of a holy man in India

8

who lived in a small hut on the bank of a river. After remaining all day in his hut, he made a ritual of emerging every day at sunset, folding his hands, and, raising his eyes in reverential wonder to the western sky, repeating, "How wonderful you are!" In deep meditation he would stand motionless, absorbing the stillness and beauty for a lengthy period.

This is an excellent spiritual practice for contemplation and meditation; through it one discovers the wonders of God, which are "more in number than grains of sand." By seeking God through wonder, the seeker is drawn to the impersonal ideal of God, and in meditation he or she strives to contact the divine Intelligence, that purely impersonal mind which governs space, time, and all the phenomena of nature. This type of contemplation is what the devotional scriptures of India term *shanta,* or a peaceful relationship to God.

Biological and anatomical studies have proved the wonders of the physical body. We can think of God as the supreme Artist who creates vast numbers of human forms, not one of which is a duplication.

We may smugly dwell on our creative abilities, but human skill falls far short of creating one delightful hummingbird. As far as is known, God has created 157 varieties of this species.

The inexhaustible Infinite is continuously bringing about creation and dissolution. Both life and death represent a cosmic drama, for change is the law of matter. Only our real Self, that is God, is unchanging and eternal. This is a further wonder of God.

God's illimitable storehouse of energy, of which there is neither beginning nor end, is yet another wonder. In the first book of the Bible we read: "And God said, 'Let there be light,' and there was light." A cosmic thought followed by material manifestation takes place with the speed of light.

God creates with complete detachment. As we develop spiritually, we also begin to share this divine detachment, which counteracts material attachment. God projected this universe and can withdraw it in the space of a heartbeat.

Further evidence of God's wonder is the human mind, which is but a pale reflection of cosmic glory. According to Indian thought, the human mind is composed of three elements: *rajas, tamas,* and *sattva.*[1] The influence of rajas shows itself when the mind is in a state of turmoil or raging with sensual desires and material distractions. Tamas makes itself felt when the mind becomes torpid, dull, and easily deluded. Sattva brings about a state of quietude, which gives us well-balanced judgment and clear understanding.

The human mind, although in a constant state of flux due to the influence of these elements, has a wide range. It spans from Shakespeare, Newton, and a host of other such luminaries to the vast majority of human beings whose abilities fall well below their level, but are nonetheless part of the Divine.

Every human mind is capable, under well-directed spiritual guidance, of rising to sublime heights; it is capable of touching the frontiers of time, space, and causality; it can emulate the majestic peace, power, and divine compassion of Jesus Christ, Buddha, or Sri Krishna.

An outstanding cause for wonder is that, of all creation, human beings alone are blessed with the divine potential to personally experience God. Even the gods, the Upanishads declare, lack this potential.

Sri Krishna reports that of all God's wonders mentioned in the tenth chapter of the Bhagavad Gita, the greatest is God becoming an individual human being. When we at last attain Self-knowledge, then we will realize that everything that was a source of wonder for us is, in fact, God made manifest. When we can lift the obscuring veil of maya, and can say, "I am He," we will emerge from our cocoon of ignorance. For us the "Divine Comedy" will have ended through contemplation on the wonder that is God.

---

[1] Sattva, rajas, and tamas are the three *gunas,* or qualities. Tamas is characterized by dullness, stupidity, and inertia; rajas by activity, restlessness, and passion; sattva by calmness, purity, and wisdom. These three qualities are found in varying proportions in the external world and in all created beings.—Ed.

THE TOUCH
OF THE HOLY

THE CONCEPT OF THE HOLY plays an important part in life. To the faithful, the idea of holiness may be associated with a variety of objects and phenomena. A person without a spiritual outlook is not inclined to regard the Bible or the Bhagavad Gita or the Koran with any special veneration. They are just books. But the case is different for a devout Christian, Hindu, or Muslim. For them the Bhagavad Gita, the Bible, and the Koran are the words of God; they are holy writings and are given special reverence.

Temples, churches, and mosques are not merely buildings for worshippers. They are holy places endowed with God's unseen presence. One should go and sit there with a pure mind.

Devout Hindus cherish a desire to visit Varanasi, Vrindaban, or Rameswaram. Many special revelations of God have occurred in these holy cities, and many saints have lived and realized God there. Similarly, Jerusalem, Bethlehem, and Mecca are holy places to Jews, Christians, and Muslims, respectively. "Put off thy shoes from off thy feet," Moses heard the voice of God say, "for the place whereupon thou standest is holy ground." A wondrous phenomenon had taken place there: a fire had been burning in a bush but the bush had remained intact. It was a miracle of God—a holy occurrence. The Jordan and Ganges are holy rivers. Mount Kailas is a holy mountain. To the Hindu, the cow is a sacred animal. Some particular days of the year or a certain point of time in a day may also be linked with the idea of the holy. Finally, there are holy men and women, holy professions, and holy actions.

If we believe in God and spiritual values, the idea of the holy is bound to affect the emotional quality of our minds. It becomes a powerful force through which we can develop purity, calmness, devotion, and spiritual insight. The touch of holiness can be important; through it even material objects can bring a glimpse of the supersensuous.

On the other hand, without a sense of holiness spiritual life can become dry and superficial. Merely attending church or visiting a temple does not bring us any tangible result. What is necessary is to contact the spirit of holiness when we are in spiritual surroundings. That is the starting point of spiritual experience.

The true spring of all holiness is, of course, God. Religions have given God various attributes: God is the Creator of this universe, God is the Supreme Being, God is the Ruler of this world, God is our Father, God is Infinite Power, and so on. But God's aspect as the Holy of Holies especially appeals to our hearts. Our lives are circumscribed by many limitations; we are constantly assailed by desires, selfishness, and ignorance. For this reason we have an innate admiration for desirelessness, complete equanimity, unselfish love, and freedom from limitations. The one name for all these qualities is holiness.

God is holy because He is unmoved by passion and unstained by any blemish. We are bound by our little individualities and fall prey to selfishness, but God's personality is cosmic so His love embraces everything. Thus, when we think of God as the Holy of Holies, we are communicating not merely with His radiant purity, but also with His infinite calm and boundless love.

The worshipper who seeks power can think of God as the Almighty. The philosopher contemplates God as the First Cause or the Omniscient Being. One who suffers from many fears seeks comfort from God the Father. But the devotee whose ideal is freedom from passions and imperfections seeks to attain a state of tranquillity, pure love, and peace; he or she meditates on God as the embodiment of holiness.

We have within us a spark of the Divine. If God is the Holy of Holies, we too have this inheritance of God's light and love. Sometimes we are not conscious of this great spiritual heritage; the Divine in us seems to be asleep. But the Divine cannot sleep forever; one day there is bound to be an awakening. The

12 object of spiritual practice is to make each of us conscious of our own divinity. Sin is not an impregnable barrier to our upliftment. Our divinity is a thousand times more powerful than our sin. Wisdom, then, is to remember our divine nature, our innate holiness, and to try to manifest this holiness in our thoughts and actions.

Great spiritual teachers never emphasize the dark side of a person's character. They know that a person's accumulated corruptions and misdeeds can be washed away by an inundation of virtue—just as dense darkness can disappear in a moment by the touch of sunlight. Sri Krishna says in the Bhagavad Gita: "Even if a man soiled with the sins of a lifetime worships God devotedly, he must be regarded as holy for he has formed the right resolution."[1] The prophet Isaiah heard the voice of God: "Though your sins be as scarlet, they shall be as white as snow."[2] We read in the Bible how Jesus Christ refused to condemn a woman who was accused by the Pharisees of having committed adultery: "And Jesus said unto her, neither do I condemn thee; go, and sin no more."[3] And Swami Vivekananda said, "Man never progresses from error to truth, but from truth to truth, from lesser truth to higher truth—but it is never from error to truth."[4] From the lives and teachings of saints and seers we get these clues of how to touch the holy.

The most important thing to remember is that the spring of holiness is the Divine within us. The purpose of spiritual practice is to gradually unfold our own divine nature. Churches, temples, books, rituals, pilgrimages, and other external holy associations enable us to feel the presence of God within.

More than churches and ceremonies, the company of holy people is a direct and effective means of imparting holiness to our lives.

Who is a holy person? One who has mastered his or her passions and selfish cravings, and who is illumined with the

---

[1] 9. 30.

[2] Isa. 1. 18.

[3] John 8. 11.

[4] *The Complete Works of Swami Vivekananda*, 8 vols. (Calcutta: Advaita Ashrama, 1976), 2: 365.

light and love of God. A holy person has attained same-sightedness toward the opposites of life. A holy person finds that the whole world glows with divine radiance. A holy person knows there is nothing that is not God.

Holy people are embodiments of joy and compassion; we are indeed fortunate when we come into contact with them. We should seek their association as often as possible, listen to their words, and serve them with love and respect. Remarkable transformations will then take place within us. Our outgoing tendencies will slowly become controlled, and our mental conflicts will gradually be resolved. Our interest in spiritual life will deepen, and we will begin to understand the true meaning of religion. Most importantly, we will be able to feel the presence of the Divine within our hearts.

Religion is not a blind adherence to certain dogmas. It is an inner experience, lifting us to a nobler level of thought, feeling, and action. Religion is a unique enrichment of our lives. Holy company can really make these things possible for us.

Another powerful influence which awakens the Divine within us is the practice of the holy name. The power of words is well known in the various secular fields of life. The same power is also effective in the spiritual field, only in a much more subtle and far-reaching way. The name of God, the mantra, when repeated with faith and reverence, generates spiritual vibrations in our bodies and minds. These vibrations purify our worldly desires. The purified and one-pointed mind can then establish contact with the indwelling Spirit, the ever-present God within us.

Holiness is God's light and love manifest in people. The deepest spring of holiness is that spiritual Reality which is the inmost core of our personalities. The objective of spiritual life is to touch that Reality. When we are able to do that, we are freed from all meanness, hatred, and delusion; we become calm, peaceful, and all-loving.

The touch of the holy makes us blessed to ourselves and to others. We then become more radiant than the ancient gods.

FREEDOM

THE IDEAL OF FREEDOM HOLDS a cherished place in human hearts, equalled in depth and intensity only by the feeling of love. To experience both is our natural state. Swami Vivekananda, the great mystic who at the turn of the century inaugurated the Vedanta movement in America, was a tireless adherent of freedom. He was fascinated by the historical account of the American struggle for freedom and independence. In his poem "To the Fourth of July," he expressed his belief that the American experiment was of spiritual origin and was the forerunner of the ultimate freedom of all oppressed peoples. So impressed was the Swami that he chose the fourth of July as the day of his passing. Much of his writing was concerned with attaining inner freedom. Thomas Jefferson, one of the leading architects of American independence, wrote, "The God who gave us life also gave us freedom." John Adams, the second president of the United States, died with the words "Independence forever" on his lips.

Significantly, death claimed both these great Americans in the same year and on the same day—the fourth of July. Jefferson and Adams were primarily concerned with the political aspect of freedom. But freedom has a much broader concept which embraces all spheres of human existence.

With the intake of our first breath, our instinctual urge for freedom is born. A babe in arms methodically advances from the crawling stage to standing, and thence to walking. Each stage symbolizes a fresh experience of freedom. The child instinctively knows when the stage of lying helpless has been outgrown and restlessly seeks action. That embryonic sense of freedom is constantly expanding; it has no end. Physical and mental growth therefore challenge any obstruction to our inherent urge for freedom.

Recently feminists have challenged the ancient Judaic male concept of God. Why should God be construed only as male—as Father? They hold that the human concept of God should include the female aspect. Statistics indicate that increasing numbers of women are joining the professional ranks and are also entering the ministry. The latter is especially true in some Protestant churches. Hence the increasing rejection of the concept of God as a solely male principle. This is a healthy sign and a symbol of the urge for freedom.

The Indian sages foresaw this identical situation thousands of years ago and formulated both the male and female aspects of God. The ancient sages depicted Shiva, the male principle, and Shakti, the female principle, as together symbolizing the concept of God where both male and female principles are equally combined. Shiva represents the tranquil, inactive state, while the female principle, Shakti, represents the dynamic aspect of God. According to ancient Hindu teachings, Shiva, the quiescent element of God's truth, and Shakti, the dynamic aspect, together represent God the Father and God the Mother; both are actually one and the same.

In the Old Testament we read that God, through Moses, gave the world the Ten Commandments. It may be asked why commandments need be given to bind human conduct. Provocative questions such as this illustrate the urge for freedom which motivates the human mind to challenge at will. Why should there be morality? Illumined sages have held that morality is not only a bulwark of freedom, but it is also instrumental for the realization of a higher and more sublime freedom. To safeguard this ideal, well-defined restrictions or moral disciplines have to be imposed. Therefore, although the Ten Commandments constitute barriers to human freedom, they bind human conduct in order to provide a higher freedom.

It is indisputable that under the guise of freedom, a form of bondage or slavery can ensue. Questions such as, Why should there be marriage? Why not enjoy free sex? are posed. In the sacred name of freedom, it is permissible for these moral concepts to be challenged. However, it would seem that queries

16

such as these are not prompted so much by clear-cut reasoning as by uncontrolled passions. Instead of freedom, one who harbors such desire is in bondage to base, animal instincts. This state of mind is the antithesis of inner freedom.

When translated from theory into practice, the noble concept of freedom is inevitably confronted by many pitfalls if not wisely and ably directed. Should it be imperfectly understood or misapplied, it inevitably degenerates into some form of slavery affecting all spheres of life.

One who craves freedom from ignorance and unwholesome passions is apt to search for God through prayer and meditation. Such a person professes to love God and claims to be a servant of God. This constitutes a form of slavery—slavery to God. But should such a seeker be taken to task on this point, a heated denial would no doubt ensue. For though this state is submission to God, it is actually a form of transcendent freedom because one who is able to sincerely love and experience God knows the highest form of freedom—freedom from the ills and sorrows of life. The seeker may feel servitude toward God by acknowledging God as master, but at the same time he or she intuitively knows that this "slavery" is raising him or her to spiritual heights through transcendental experience. Such a devotee is released from bondage to passions such as hatred, violence, pride, and jealousy. The limitations to freedom which the ignorant experience on the material plane are nonexistent to devotees of God.

A voluntary curtailment of freedom is vital in order for greater freedom to ensue. One of the most far-reaching truths that India has revealed to the world is that all human beings are basically and eternally free—free from all bondage, whether of space, time, natural laws, moral obligations, and/or the bondage of religious worship. However, the realization of this blessing is not immediate. One must spiritually evolve through barriers to freedom such as moral and religious disciplines. These involve prayer, worship, and meditation.

From a spiritual standpoint, the created universe itself constitutes bondage. The realization of the implications of this bondage and its far-reaching effects is a slow and arduous process. For example, political bondage, social barriers, and inordinate attachments are but a few threats to inner freedom. A spiritually evolved person becomes ever more conscious of the insidious subtleties of material bondage. This great revelation, however, is denied to those who are not on the spiritual path. They are deluded by the material senses which are treacherous and unreliable. One of the results of spiritual growth is the realization that bondage to the material senses poses the greatest threat to our inner freedom.

A dedicated follower of the spiritual path challenges his or her own body much as Saint Francis of Assisi did when he aspired to higher experiences of God. In this respect he found his physical body a great handicap. When he wished to meditate he felt drowsy; when he wanted to pray, his body clamored for food. He would soundly berate his body, calling it "Brother Ass." Conversely he would say, "Well, Brother, you have cooperated so you shall have food today." The food consisted of weak lentil soup, the main constituent of Saint Francis' meager diet.

All material existence is characterized by constant change. This being so, a dedicated seeker senses an underlying threat to freedom in the existent life plan. In a mystical mood, Shakespeare put the following words on the lips of a dying soldier, philosophizing on the futility of the world's sham:

> But thought's the slave of life, and life time's fool;
> And time, that takes survey of all the world,
> Must have a stop.[1]

As Shakespeare observed, the mind is but a tool of life; it is not the ultimate. Through our powerful spiritual potential, we can subdue and overcome the mind. The mind is only a servant of human life, but without its guidance life would be impossible. Again, life itself is not independent, being in turn the slave of time.

Ages ago there was no life on this planet; life evolved from a cosmic source at a later, specific stage of evolution. Time, then, is more powerful than life. There is a school of scientific thought which holds that at some distant time there will be no

[1] *1 Henry IV* 5. 4. 80-82.

18 life on this planet. The solar system, indispensable to life, will cease to be. Shakespeare's lines, then, pose a challenge: Is there anything more powerful than time?

The innermost soul of humanity replies in the affirmative. We can overcome time, for time "must have a stop." This is not idle speculation. Dedicated followers of truth have been known to stop time. When does time stop? It stops in the realm of the Infinite. The infinite Self is not subject to time; the Self nullifies time. Time and space are mere projections of, and confined to, the human self on the material plane. Infinite Consciousness, which is our own true nature, is totally independent of anything belonging to space, time, or causation. According to Vedanta, God has an absolute nature and that nature is above the personal God on whom dedicated human beings meditate and pray.

Spiritual progress is marked by specific stages; there is no royal road or shortcut. The way is hard and long, requiring strict, supervised discipline. Then slowly but surely, through patient dedicated worship, meditation, and prayer, spiritual development gradually occurs. This stage is reached by worshipping God faithfully as the God of infinite love, power, and compassion. Complete freedom from one's lower animal nature inevitably results.

When this sublime stage is reached, we realize that God has guided our lives. Being adjudged ready, we become the recipients of a higher spiritual experience. God now reveals Himself as absolute Truth. It is at this stage that freedom in the truest sense becomes a reality. We feel unity with everything and are no longer identified with the physical body; we become one with God the Absolute.

GOD
AND HIS MAYA

ALTHOUGH MANY OF US ARE familiar with the word "maya,"
we are sometimes confused about its meaning and significance.
In the Indian spiritual tradition, the word maya is used in different ways.

The vast universe—with its living beings and all its phenomena—exists and functions because of God. God is behind
everything. Maya is God's own power, the great cosmic power
through which God operates the three cosmic processes of creation, sustenance, and dissolution. God has been called *Mayi*,
the Master of maya.

For the lover of God, maya is not terrifying. It is God's play.
For example, if we love a child and the child jumps and plays,
we are not fearful or displeased. The child doesn't need to be
always quiet.

God is infinite and beyond our limited understanding. Do
we have full knowledge even of ourselves? We are aware of our
own bodies, minds, desires, and emotions, but there are areas of
ourselves that remain dark mysteries to us. How foolish it is,
then, to ask about the workings of an infinite God! We cannot
understand why God plays the way He does.

And His play is not all joy. Everything doesn't happen
according to our wishes. Some things we find pleasant, while
others are not to our liking. We are in this world to face different situations in our lives. But if we are devotees of God, we
should remember that it is all God's maya, God's play. Joy or
sorrow, health or sickness, life or death, beauty or ugliness—
whatever we see is part of His cosmic sport. And, as the

devotee's goal is to experience God, he or she need not bother about maya. We need to love God and have faith in God, experiencing Him both in our lives and in the outside world.

For the devotee, maya is very real; it is a real manifestation of God's power which continually surrounds us. By God's grace the devotee can rise above maya and feel God's presence. If we can experience God, maya cannot entangle us. Even when death comes we shall see the sweet face of God through the frowning face of maya. When the experience of God-consciousness comes, maya—though real—cannot affect us.

Such is the attitude of devotees or, philosophically speaking, dualists. They say, "I am God's devotee. I am seeking God, and this world is God's play. He is infinite." These are the simple concepts by which devotees lead their spiritual lives.

For nondualists, the goal is to find the Supreme Unity. This world of multiplicity and its endless manifestations—beginning with space and time, and appearing as matter, energy, life, and mind—all hide the truth of Unity. Unity is the goal for seekers of knowledge; their goal is to attain the supreme nondualistic Reality, the One without a second. This is my true Self. Space, time, body, mind, life—everything is merged in that supreme unity of the Self.

For such seekers, what, then, is maya? Maya is the constantly changing, self-contradictory principle of existence; it cannot be described as real or unreal. Maya is inscrutable. It is real for some time, but when analyzed, disappears like a dream.

The most absurd things occur in dreams, but as long as the dream lasts, it seems real. Only when we wake up does the dream become unreal, a creation of the mind. In the same manner, the nondualist says, every experience—gross or subtle—has a dual nature. It appears to exist, but when critically analyzed, it disappears into the Self. For the person who has attained this experience, the Self is the only reality: existence comes from the Self, knowledge comes from the Self, joy also comes from the Self. The nondualist, or *advaitin,* says that maya exists, but it is not real. Maya has to be ignored. Just as darkness disappears when the sun rises, so maya disappears when the knowledge of the Self dawns.

In the beginning, Vedanta tells us to be very discriminating, stubborn, and careful about maya, because maya hides the truth of *Brahman* and projects multiplicity.[1] We are seeking the One, but the manifold appears before us all the time. We have to be intolerant of maya in the early stage of our spiritual search. Maya is all around us. The very moment we say, "I am eating," we are in maya. The very moment we see a flower, we are in maya.

The spiritual seeker has to be very austere and uncompromising with maya. One needs the kind of discrimination that counsels: This is all maya; this is all a dream; this is not real. But as spiritual understanding develops, the seeker realizes that whatever exists is nothing but the Self.

Every part of the universe has existence. Where does it come from? From that infinite existence, Brahman. Everything that we experience has knowledge associated with it. Everything shines with knowledge. Whenever a thought arises in the mind, we are conscious of that thought. When we see a mountain, we are conscious of the mountain. Consciousness is attached to everything. Vedantins, therefore, try to see that all things are pieces of Consciousness. The manifold universe is grounded in and permeated by the Infinite as Consciousness. Existence and Consciousness are the two faces of the one Reality—Brahman, or *Atman*.[2]

When we begin to understand that, our attitude begins to change. We are no longer intolerant; we develop strong detachment along with the strength to try to see the Self, or Brahman, in everything.

The formula given in the Chandogya Upanishad is: *Sarvam khalvidam Brahma*, "All this is Brahman." At this stage we give up the distinction between maya and Brahman. Maya is God. It is God who has projected the manifold out of Himself, and it is God who has entered into everything.

---

[1] Brahman is the all-pervading divine Existence, the Ground of the universe.—Ed.

[2] Atman is the divine Spirit within us, the Self which is one with Brahman.—Ed.

SEEING GOD EVERYWHERE: A PRACTICAL GUIDE TO SPIRITUAL LIVING

22   Vedanta tells us that since the ultimate Reality is one, whatever is seen or experienced is truly that same Reality. When
Brahman, or the true Self, is realized, maya merges into the Self.
In the deepest state of meditation, or *samadhi*, there is no duality; there is only the One.[3] It cannot even be said to be One; it
is the indescribable experience of the nondual Truth.

After coming down from samadhi, the seer remembers that
unitary experience and knows that maya is not separate from
Brahman. Later, when the experience of the Self becomes
stable, he or she tangibly feels that the manifold is really the
Self. It is the Self that has become space, time, matter, life, and
mind. Everything that is seen and experienced is nothing but
the Self.

In an integrated spiritual life, these different attitudes and
approaches are useful. When we are in a devotional mood, we
should look upon maya with love. "Oh, how wonderful is God's
creation, God's play!" God is not an ordinary player. He is playing with beauty and with ugliness. Maya thrills the devotee; he
or she sees God's glory in maya. When we are in a devotional
mood, we have to accept His creation, His maya, His play, His
cosmic power and manifestation.

In the mood of nondualism, we think that maya is not real.
We say, "I will have nothing to do with maya. I am seeking the
unity within my Self." Detachment and discrimination are necessary because we are involved with maya. Forgetting the spiritual Reality, we have become captivated by maya's spell.

Maya has two functions: to bind, *avidya maya*, and to
liberate, *vidya maya*. At a certain stage, maya binds us and we
forget the spiritual Reality which is the goal of life. We don't
know why we are acting, moving about, and struggling in this
world; we have become prisoners. This is the binding, captivat-
ing power of maya. Then a time comes when we see this and
we want to get out. Maya then cooperates. How? Through spiritual practices: meditation, prayer, holy company, study of the

---

[3] Samadhi is the highest state of spiritual realization in which a person experiences his or her own identity with the ultimate Reality.—Ed.

scriptures, and mental discipline. All these things are within the realm of maya, but they are vidya maya, which liberates us.

In the beginning, we feel weak compared to the vast power of maya. We feel helpless and so pray to God, the Ruler of maya, from whom maya has come. The seeker in the Isa Upanishad prays, "The face of truth is hidden by thy golden orb, O Sun. Do thou remove it, in order that I, who am devoted to truth, may behold its glory."[4]

In the path of devotion, our goal is God; in the path of knowledge, the goal is our true Self. Ultimately, both are the same. We need not be afraid of maya. Maya has to be understood and overcome. The body, mind, and ego are expressions of maya. From the highest standpoint, these are not necessary— the true Self does not need to eat or have diversions—but since the Self has been imprisoned in a body, there is no end to our needs and desires. This is the play of maya.

When we become aware of this predicament, we long for real freedom and then maya helps us to attain freedom. When we can see the inherent contradictions of life, the desire to rise above maya becomes intensified. God and His maya then join together. There is no maya in the formless Brahman. He is beyond mind and words; He is indescribable.

When we have found our own true nature, that of effulgent Light, there is no longer any maya. Then we find that there is no difference between the highest truth of God and the highest truth of an individual being. Thus, the Upanishads proclaim, "I am Brahman. Thou art That." This is the highest goal, where there is no more maya, and we are ever free.

---

[4] Verse 15.

LIVING INWARDLY

IN MY EVERYDAY LIFE IT is not necessary to have a comprehensive knowledge of my internal world. And even if I am interested in it, I have to gather information about it from the external world. Don't I have to study anatomy and physiology in bodies that are not my own? Don't I have to learn the workings of the mind by studying other people's minds? So it seems that I pursue most of the values of my life in the external world. My internal world, while an integral part of my existence, merely functions as a means to utilize and enjoy the external. It doesn't matter if I give only a minimum of attention to it, for, as an average person, I consciously live almost completely in the outer world.

Under these circumstances, inward living cannot be of interest to average people; it seems not only unnecessary, but fanciful and strange. Their only knowledge of inward living is that of the psychopath who withdraws from the objective world and lives entirely in self-created fantasies. So much has been written about such abnormal behavior that many have become suspicious of any kind of contemplative life. They even dislike inwardly directed religion. Thus they choose a religion that is no more than a social force, a behavior pattern which must operate in the workaday world like any other element of outward conduct. Many regard the mystical tradition in religion with contempt and correlate it with psychological immaturity.

The Katha Upanishad explains:

> God made man's senses pointed outward from his very birth, so that man always looks outside of himself and never within. Extremely rare is that wise person, who, desiring immortality, directs his senses inward and perceives the truth of his own innermost Self.[1]

---

[1] 2. 1. 1.

But the rarity of a phenomenon should not cause it to be labelled either as absurd or as nonexistent. In the field of science, sometimes far-reaching knowledge has been deduced from a single and extremely difficult experiment. This is especially true in the science of spiritual knowledge. To attain spiritual truth we must be prepared for unusual undertakings. We should not be discouraged simply because this is not the way chosen by average worldly people.

The unusual endeavors through which we seek to unravel the ultimate mysteries within our lives and personalities may be called inward living. Who am I? Why am I here? What is the meaning of this life? Why do I have to struggle this way? What is my place in this vast universe surrounding me? At certain moments in our lives these and other profound questions trouble us and we want clear answers. We are not satisfied with mere intellectual speculations.

According to Vedanta, it is possible to find unequivocal answers to these questions by directly experiencing the reality of God. This kind of experience requires a suitable adjustment in our way of understanding. A shift of emphasis must be made from the external to the internal world; it requires a reorientation of our living habits. Within the core of our personalities, says Vedanta, is a spiritual Reality. It is birthless and deathless, unlimited by time, space, and causality. It is infinite Consciousness and infinite Bliss. Far from the common view that supersensuous experience is not normal, it is the *empirical* life which is aberrant, a dislocation from a spiritual state of perfection.

Let us not be caught up in such questions as how this common aberration got started. This question is quite unimportant. For us, the important thing is to discover the truth. And Vedanta assures us that this discovery can be made here and now. The concluding verse of the Katha Upanishad says:

> Having received this wisdom taught by the King of Death, and the entire process of yoga, Nachiketa became free from impurities and death and attained Self-knowledge. Thus it will also be with any other who knows the inmost Self.[2]

---

[2] 2. 3. 18.

26   Any person, then, having the courage, patience, and perseverance to carry on the experiment can hope to attain Self-knowledge. Again, Self-knowledge is, in the language of the Mundaka Upanishad, "the foundation of all knowledge." The individual's center is identical with the center of the universe. In the last analysis, the true nature of what we call the outside world is spiritual. In the vision of truth, the external and internal are only arbitrary divisions of what is one continuous, indivisible Reality—the Spirit.

The Taittiriya Upanishad speaks of the five *koshas,* or sheaths, which cover the Self. They are, as it were, five screens which prevent our vision of the Self. The technique of inward living gradually removes these sheaths, allowing us to attain the eternal Ground of existence, the core of the personality, our true Self. The first covering is the physical body, the *annamaya kosha.* A person's consciousness is almost always centered in the body. When I say "I," I mean my body. The identification of consciousness with the body is so natural and complete that it seems almost impossible to challenge it. Yet this extrication of the "I" sense from the body can be achieved, and to the extent that we achieve it, we are prepared for the experience of higher truth.

The second covering of the Self is the *pranamaya kosha,* the totality of the vital energies responsible for the various physiological functions within our bodies. When I say "I am breathing" or "I am digesting food," I identify with two forms of this vital energy called *prana.*[3] The Upanishads prescribe various meditations on prana for the purpose of raising one's consciousness from the body to a higher level of the life-force. Those who can identify with that powerhouse of energy attain great control over the body; they spontaneously experience a new feeling of freedom, strength, and joy. Consciousness on the level of the pranamaya kosha is subtler and more powerful than that of the first covering, the annamaya kosha.

Next comes the mental sheath, the *manomaya kosha.* This is the portion of the mind that receives impulses from the external world through the senses and then sorts them.

---

[3] Prana is the vital breath that sustains life and manifests as thought, bodily function, and physical action.—Ed.

The fourth sheath, the *vijnanamaya kosha,* brings these processes to a conclusion. *Vijnana* means "certain knowledge"; it includes the three mental activities of feeling, willing, and knowing. In the manomaya kosha, thoughts have not yet taken a specific shape; they are vague, amorphous, and hence ineffective. But on the level of the vijnanamaya kosha, the nature of the ideas has been determined, and the resulting clear knowledge is ready to be connected with action. The vijnanamaya kosha has been translated as the "intelligence sheath." The manomaya and vijnanamaya sheaths together constitute what we call the mind.

The Upanishads have clearly distinguished the mind from the prana, or the life-force, and special meditations have been described that teach us to be deeply conscious of ourselves as thinking and creative beings. Shifting the center of the personality from the body and life-force to the mind opens up new channels of superior wisdom. Yet the mind, both in its role of accumulating and in clearly determining ideas, is only a sheath—a covering concealing our true nature.

As we expand awareness from the body to the vital energy and the mind, we must know that we are more than just thinking beings. The fifth covering is the *anandamaya kosha,* the blissful sheath. This is the element which contributes joy to our experiences. The many kinds of pleasures and satisfactions that we derive from the wide range of our activities all come from this sheath of bliss. As we detach consciousness from the four previous sheaths and approach the fifth one, the experience of bliss becomes more intense, and the gross delights which come from sights, sounds, and tastes are left behind in the experience of subtle joys which do not require external stimuli.

What is beyond this fifth sheath? The Atman—the Self, the personality's true center. The Atman witnesses all the experiences that come through the five sheaths. It is pure awareness. All that we know through our sense organs or mental processes is known because of the innermost Self within. It sits quietly behind the five screens and radiates Consciousness through all these layers. The Atman is the true subject of all experience. It is infinitely more than the physical body or the vital force or the mind and intelligence or all these put together.

28   When we discover the inner Self, which is our true nature, our lives completely change. We can then no longer use the term "inner life." It was only for starting the journey to the Self that we had to speak of living inwardly: from the standpoint of the Self there is no such distinction as inner and outer. We use these terms with reference to the body. Once we realize the Self we find that everything rests in the Self. This whole universe with all its multiplicity is nothing but an expression of the consciousness of the Self. At this stage the seeker is able to say, "This universe is resting in me and I am in everything. I am one with this universe. Self-knowledge is the realization of the oneness of my own truth and all the truth outside of me."

In order to discover our true Self—the Ground of our existence—we have to practice detachment from the non-Self, which is comprised of the five sheaths. By the practice of detachment no flight from life is meant; rather it means a sober, calm, and unbiased attitude toward the objects and events around us and in us. Those who aspire to knowledge should fulfill their duties and responsibilities as well as they can, but they should keep themselves free from over-involvement in any situation. They should not place too much hope on anything in this perpetual flux of events. They should not forget that the goal of life is to realize the eternal truth, the true Self.

In this realization alone can we understand what this life means. All our deeper questions become clear only when we discover ourselves as pure Spirit. The state of Self-knowledge is described by the Chandogya Upanishad thus: "I am below. I am above. I am behind. I am in front. I am in the south. I am in the north. I am all that is."[4] And again:

> From the one I pervade the many. From the many I go to the one. Shaking off all imperfections as a horse shakes dust from its hair, freeing myself from body-consciousness . . . I who have realized my true Self am now identified with Brahman, the Supreme Reality.[5]

---

[4] 7. 25.
[5] 8. 13.

THE HEALING
POWER OF SILENCE

EVERY ONE OF US HAS probably felt the beneficial influence of silence. Even the busiest people need to have breaks of silence in their work. Silence seems to be a necessary factor in our lives, yet we do not always realize the implications of the quietness we unconsciously seek and enjoy when we take a walk in a solitary meadow or in a forest or on a mountain. These quiet recreations may not occur very often, but when they do we cannot forget the spell that such solitary communion with nature leaves upon us.

Again, if we chance to wake up at dead of night when everything is calm around us, the deep silence of the night seems to penetrate into our being. Of course, silence may be frightening: some people cannot bear the absence of sound. But apart from those few, most of us welcome and profit by occasional contacts of silence in nature or even in our homes. Our nerves are soothed, energy is regained, and the total effect is bracing to our bodies and minds.

The experience of deep sleep proves our need for silence. We may be very busy throughout the day, but at night we hanker for that hour when everything—our sense perceptions, responsibilities, thoughts, worries, emotions, desires, hopes—is left behind. What is sleep? Is it not silence? In sleep nothing disturbs us. Even though we leave everything behind, including body consciousness, we enjoy the experience.

However, sleep is not emptiness. The sages of the Upanishads had great insight into the study of sleep. According to them, sleep leads human consciousness close to the Ground of universal Existence, which is infinite calmness. That is why, when we come back to the waking state, we return refreshed and at peace.

God has combined noise and silence, activity and rest; it is the plan of nature. Look at the boundless space outside. Scientists say that space is vast, containing millions and millions of stars with their planets, galactic systems, and nebulae. Yet this stellar universe is very small compared to the immensity of empty space. If by some cosmic disorder all the celestial bodies were to collide and be annihilated, the vastness of space would not be affected in the least. And what is this vast space? Is it not characterized by an immeasurable silence?

Imagine the totality of sounds emerging from this small planet of ours, the summation of all the noises produced every minute by millions and millions of human beings and all other kinds of living creatures and machines, as well as various natural phenomena. Then think of a similar noise connected with every other heavenly body. If we now add all these noises together, we can imagine what an enormous quantity of sound this cosmic universe can produce. Yet compared to the infinite stillness of space, this sound is nothing. Throughout the universe there is great activity; there are innumerable interactions throughout life, mind, and energy on one side of the picture, but there is also another side. Behind all these cosmic activities there is the vast silence of limitless space and time.

Time, like space, is inexhaustible. Like a river it flows continuously, without any regard for what happens within it. Thus space and time are both silent sentinels of these cosmic activities which we call the world processes. That is the plan of God. If God is responsible for this plan of creation, His plan includes not only evolution and activity, but also a state of quiescence that pervades the vastness of space and time.

All this refers to external silence, the quietude of our surroundings. It is necessary for every one of us in the interest of our physical and mental health to consciously avail ourselves of silence as much as we can, apart from the rest we obtain from sleep. A person can try a preliminary practice of silence by just sitting quietly without any serious thought or activity. To be by oneself, if only for ten minutes, is a healthy tonic for our physical health, but this practice also serves to relieve our cares, anxieties, and mental restlessness. One can sometimes get up at 3:00 a.m., when everything is still, and try to feel the pulse of the serene night. It will have a remarkably soothing effect on the mind.

More important than outward silence is inward silence, and that is not so easily available to us. Just as when we look outside and see a vast universe interwoven with activities and quietude, our internal world has both action and silence. When we look into the mind we ordinarily see only the surface phenomena—thoughts, feelings, and desires. We must make additional effort to experience that inner silence, the silence of the mind; we must silence our inordinate desires and passions. The background of silence escapes our notice. If we can come in touch with that inner realm of silence, our mental troubles can be healed.

Without such healing, the unrest and suffering caused by maladjustments, unbridled passions, desires, and frustrations can result in illness. We have to seek the counsel of psychiatrists who may or may not be able to help us. Driven by psychological complexes, we feel restless. Repressions and unsatisfied urges can fragment our personalities; when this occurs, the mind becomes a great burden—an uncontrollable enemy with which we cannot cope. Both our foolishness and wrong education have created the mind's restless behavior. The remedy must come from within ourselves: the remedy lies in the discovery of the true background of the personality.

Here is a simple practice for experiencing inner calmness: it consists of watching the mind and trying to see what is going on within. This practice is not necessarily spiritual; we need not remember God or meditate on a spiritual idea. All we have to do is just sit quietly and observe the movement of our thoughts. As we observe the mind, we place ourselves outside the mind for the time being. We should not allow ourselves to be involved with the ideas that appear and disappear on the mental scene. We need not feel mortified if some bad thoughts come. Neither should we be elated if good thoughts appear. We are neutral spectators, as it were. In itself, watching the mind will gradually lead us to the experience of inner silence. We will find that thoughts are no longer rushing in in an irregular way. Our nerves will be soothed, and our minds will attain considerable stability and a new power of self-control.

Next we can substitute simple "watching" with an active effort to concentrate. In general, concentration means fixing the mind on a particular object without allowing it to wander from thought to thought. The mind in its ignorant state is always restless. It is continually being pulled by sense objects outside and agitated by desires and attachments inside. This restless state of mind can be controlled by the practice of concentration.

But a spiritual perspective in this practice is essential if we wish to reach the quiescent Consciousness that illumines our bodies, minds, and the world of our experience. The objects selected for meditation may differ, according to the temperament of the aspirant. It is easy for some to concentrate upon an image. Others find it more convenient to focus their minds on a spiritual idea or a word-symbol, a mantra. The goal of concentration, however, is the same in all cases; namely, to reach the Ground of our being, the Self. To the extent that we can do this, we proportionately develop mental composure, strength, and peace.

Spiritual life is essentially a life of silence. It means learning to experience deepening, chastening states of inner quietude. What does love of God imply? Experiencing that calmness which can cure our ignorance. The more we love God, the more we become silent in the spiritual sense. There is no longer any "noise" from the turbulent mind. In the Upanishads, God is described as *Shivam shantam,* the essence of goodness, the essence of silence.

The more we approach God through love, the feebler our worldly attachments become. We become transformed through the touch of divine love. No longer do we suffer from the clamor of infatuation, hatred, or wild desires. The whole world becomes transfigured for us.

Love for God makes our lives quiet. Not that we become like stone; spiritual tranquillity is not inertia. It is marked by the highest wisdom and clarity of insight. External noise and perplexities do not disturb us anymore; we find harmony and peace. The whole world's tremendous activity appears to us to be the silent play of God.

The healing power of spiritual silence can also be found through unselfish actions. If we can dedicate our actions to God without considering ourselves the doers or the enjoyers of work, then this detached attitude serves to make us calm and creates an abiding calmness in the background of our lives. It is essentially an eternal, spiritual truth shining in its own majesty. Though we are always living in this truth, it remains veiled by our ego-sense, our false individuality. Unselfish action gradually tears this veil until we are given a vision of that "peace that passeth all understanding."

Finally, there is the Vedantic way of approaching the silence of our being through reflective analysis of the "seer and the seen." We read in the Upanishads, "This Atman is eternally silent."[1] The Atman, our true Self, is the eternal subject, the "seer," and everything else is the object, the "seen." What we call movement—noise, distraction, or activities—all belong to the realm of objective experience. Behind this objective experience there is the eternal Witness which is our true Self, and the more we grasp this fact, the more we partake of the nature of the Self. By separating the subject from the object, we can eventually become centered in the Self. The Atman is never an object of thought. Nothing can disturb its silent majesty. It precedes all other facts.

The Atman, the basic, eternal Existence and Consciousness, is the primary fact of existence; everything else follows. When I am poised in the Atman, even my body is external to me. My mind, thoughts, and movements are all outside of me. This is the process of reflective analysis. In monistic Vedanta we call the process *neti, neti,* "not this, not this." We have to push away everything that is not the Self. We must be extremely selfish in the spiritual sense; that is, we must know that in the Self there is no place for any other thing. Of course, this is not the final picture of truth. However, when we are trying to realize the Self, we have to practice this kind of sternness because in our perception the subject and the object have become mixed together, and this has created all our troubles. It is like a

---

[1] Katha 1. 3. 13.

34 malignant tumor that needs immediate surgery. The surgical treatment is not a cruel act; the surgeon is my friend for he is saving my life. In the basic malady of life the Self has become confused with the non-Self, and, as the result of this spiritual "tumor," we are full of wrong ideas. So in Vedanta we say, "I am not this, I am not this."

Then when we discover our true Self, we find that it can never actually be confused with the non-Self. No illness, no passion, no death, no frustration, no suffering can ever disturb the eternal stillness of the Self. That is the end of all ignorance, or maya. We have reached the center of tranquillity, the source of infinite security and happiness. We have attained the culmination of healing by being one with Silence, untouched by any noise or imperfection.

When we finally know this truth, we will also know that what we had previously eliminated as not being part of us is actually within us. There is no such thing as duality. There is only one homogeneous unity, and that is the Self. Distinctions of external and internal vanish at that stage, and it is no longer necessary to call the Self "silence" because without the opposition of noise, or movements, there cannot be any concept of "silence."

Everything that is, is *in* the Self. Everything *is* the Self. Whatever names and words and ideas we use are included in the Self. That is the highest truth, and the steps to that highest truth are to be gained through the experiences of the different kinds of silence, beginning with external silence. Through all these stages, silence becomes a progressively greater healing power in our lives until ultimately it reaches its culmination in the Truth, which is our true Self.

"Dive Deep,"
Said Sri Ramakrishna

SPIRITUAL PROGRESS DEPENDS TO A considerable extent upon one's earnest personal endeavor. "Arise, awake! Approach the wise teachers and learn from them," the Katha Upanishad says.[1] Throughout the Bhagavad Gita we find Sri Krishna exhorting his disciple Arjuna in a similar strain: "O mighty descendant of Bharata, arise; shake off all doubt and hesitation and hold fast to the practice of yoga."[2] Again Christ says, "Ask and it shall be given you, seek and ye shall find, knock and it shall be opened unto you."[3] Jesus is clearly stating the primary requirements for a spiritual aspirant: a keen desire and an ardent striving for the spiritual ideal. The same voice has been heard once again in our own age in this simple teaching from Sri Ramakrishna: "Dive deep."

Sri Ramakrishna took this expression from two popular Bengali religious songs in which the spiritual quest has been compared to the search for precious gems at the bottom of the sea. One of the songs begins thus:

> Dive deep, O mind, dive deep in the Ocean of God's Beauty;
> If you descend to the uttermost depths,
> There you will find the gem of Love.[4]

---

[1] 1. 3. 14.

[2] 4. 42.

[3] Mt. 7. 7.

[4] M, *The Gospel of Sri Ramakrishna,* trans. Swami Nikhilananda (New York: Ramakrishna-Vivekananda Center, 1952), p. 153.

36 The second song opens in this manner:

> Taking the name of Kali, dive deep down, O mind,
> Into the heart's fathomless depths,
> Where many a precious gem lies hid.
> But never believe the bed of the ocean bare of gems
> If in the first few dives you fail;
> With firm resolve and self-control
> Dive deep and make your way to Mother Kali's realm.[5]

The two simple words "dive deep" are an incentive to engage in spiritual struggle. Sri Ramakrishna used them as a stimulus for devotees to take up spiritual practices with all their strength.

Those blessed persons who have realized the Truth do not speak in the sophisticated jargon of scholars; their language is straight and penetrating, their appeal is not to the imagination but to prompt and effective action. "Dive deep" is an excellent example of this. It is interesting to note that Sri Ramakrishna employed this simple maxim as a powerful corrective to three principal religious aberrations that he observed.

The first of these can be called a superficial fidelity to religion. Vast is the difference between make-believe formality in the name of religion and a genuine spiritual hankering. When we do not care to know the true meaning and goal of religion and consider it merely a customary fashion, then religion loses its spiritual power either for the individual or society. It becomes just a series of mechanical activities in a temple or a church—a bundle of idle speculations on the life beyond, or some unquestioned ritual, performed because of some vague, otherworldly fear.

True spiritual hankering is very different from this kind of confused thinking and behavior. Whenever a great religious teacher has appeared, his first duty has been to point out the difference between lifeless customs and a living fervor for spiritual life. This was evident in Buddha when he denounced the traditional followers of the religious patterns of his time. The

---

[5] *Gospel*, p. 124.

Bhagavad Gita shows that Sri Krishna also made the distinction between genuine spiritual seeking and formal religion based on ritualistic sacrifices. In the case of Jesus, we know that before he chose his disciples and began to preach his message, he first prepared the ground by rebuking the Sadducees and Pharisees. In his spiritual ministration Sri Ramakrishna also had to face the same problem: for the most part, people have only a superficial religious allegiance. This is our primary spiritual perversity. "Dive deep" was his solution. In the *Gospel of Sri Ramakrishna* we find numerous instances of the saint's eloquently drawing the distinction between formal piety and an honest spiritual quest. For religion to be a mighty fact of life rather than a futile conjecture, its votaries must "dive deep."

It was not that Sri Ramakrishna did not recognize the value of rituals and customary religious observances in certain contexts, but compared to the ultimate goal of life—the realization of God—formal religion was, according to him, of little worth. "God can be seen," Sri Ramakrishna said. "He can be touched. We can even talk with God." He is the most essential power in our lives, the most important element in our thoughts, aspirations, and actions. We may cite one simple illustration that Sri Ramakrishna used to give: When you add zeros successively to the digit one, you get figures whose value increases proportionately: a hundred, a thousand, a million, etc., while any number of zeros without the digit one before them are of no value. Similarly, God is the numeral one in all the values of life. If you leave Him out of the picture in life's pursuits, those pursuits become a string of worthless zeros.

We may recall a portion of the interesting conversation between Sri Ramakrishna and Pundit Iswar Chandra Vidyasagar, the great scholar, philanthropist, and educational pioneer of Bengal. One day Sri Ramakrishna went to visit the pundit, and, as was his custom, the Master soon gave their conversation a spiritual turn. In a mood of eloquent inspiration Sri Ramakrishna emphasized the difference between a moral or even a virtuous life on the one hand, and a genuine hankering for God-realization on the other. He said to Vidyasagar:

> The activities that you are engaged in are good. It is
> very good if you can perform them in a selfless

38

spirit, renouncing egotism, giving up the idea that you are the doer. . . .

The more you come to love God, the less you will be inclined to perform action. When the daughter-in-law is with child, her mother-in-law gives her less work to do. . . . There is gold buried in your heart, but you are not yet aware of it. It is covered with a thin layer of clay. Once you are aware of it, all these activities of yours will lessen.[6]

Swami Vivekananda reiterated his Master's sentiment when he said that religion should not be looked upon as a Japanese vase in one's drawing room. Such a vase is only one of the many decorations one has in the house in order to pass oneself off as cultured. Similarly, religion may be just one of the various interests we have in order to pose as "decent" people. Do we not make religion a kind of mockery with such an attitude? Most of the criticisms that have been leveled against religion are due to the fact that the majority of people who pass as "religious" do not show any higher behavior than a superficial allegiance to the faith they profess. If a case for religion is to be presented, it can be done only by the practical example of sincere people who are ready to "dive deep."

When Sri Ramakrishna said, "Dive deep," he was careful to describe the full implications of this phrase. "Now dive deep into the Ocean of God. There is no fear of death from plunging into this Ocean, for this is the Ocean of Immortality,"[7] he assured us. We have nothing to fear from the spiritual struggle. It will not land us in darkness and uncertainty. The sacrifices we make during spiritual practice will be more than compensated when we become illumined.

The second religious aberration that Sri Ramakrishna noticed was the confusion of spiritual wisdom with intellectual sophistry. For many people religion is equated with a sort of intellectual understanding of the scriptures or system of philosophy. Their emphasis is on argumentation rather than on actual

---

[6] *Gospel*, p. 108.

[7] *Gospel*, pp. 455-56.

practice, on reading books rather than on contemplation. An intellectual grasp of religious issues is, of course, good. But here great caution is necessary. Sri Ramakrishna liked to illustrate the folly of mere religious intellectualism by likening it to counting the leaves, trees, and branches of a mango orchard. Such idle counting is foolishness. It is wiser to eat the mangoes. Similarly, since the aim of human birth is to love God, one should seek to attain that love and be at peace. "What need is there of your knowing the infinite qualities of God? You may discriminate for millions of years about God's attributes, and still you will not know them."[8]

If by blessed fortune one happens to take an interest in religion, that interest should not be frittered away in mere theoretical estimations. "Dive deep" would be Sri Ramakrishna's pronouncement to these theoreticians; religion does not consist of books, but in transforming the words of books into living truth.

To recall another simple illustration that Sri Ramakrishna used to give: Suppose you have to purchase certain things from the market. While at home you prepare a list of the articles you want. After you have made the purchases, the list ceases to be of value; you may as well discard it. In a way, the scriptures are like this list. Their purpose is to indicate the means to realize the Truth. Once you are on the path, however, it becomes a waste of time to inordinately cling to them. It is more important to plunge into spiritual practice.

Sri Ramakrishna's conversation with one of the celebrities of his time, Pundit Shashadhar Tarkachudamani, is illuminating in this connection. The author "M" records the Master as having said the following words to the pundit:

> There are many scriptures like the Vedas. But one cannot realize God without austerity and spiritual discipline. . . .
>
> Better than reading is hearing. . . . But seeing is far better than hearing. Then all doubts disappear. It is true that many things are recorded in the scriptures;

---

[8] *Gospel*, p. 463.

40

but all these are useless without the direct realization of God, without devotion to His Lotus Feet, without purity of heart.[9]

The pundit had taken upon himself the task of preaching the principles of Hinduism to various social gatherings. His fascinating talks used to draw crowds—a fact of which the Master was well aware. He asked the pundit if he had received a commission from the Lord to preach. When the pundit replied in the negative, Sri Ramakrishna told him that unless he had realized the Truth and had actually received the Lord's commission, his preaching would be a waste of breath. In conclusion, the Master repeated his formula, "Dive deep." Continuing in this vein, Sri Ramakrishna added, "My child, add a little more to your strength. Practice spiritual discipline a few days more. You have hardly set your foot on the tree, yet you expect to lay hold of a big cluster of fruit."[10]

The third aberration that Sri Ramakrishna was at pains to correct was a lukewarm attitude toward spiritual practice. Some people realize the importance of spiritual disciplines and also understand the difference between a mere intellectual interest in religion and a real longing to realize God. Yet for some reason they cannot exert themselves as much as they should. As Sri Ramakrishna put it, they are "lukewarm." Lukewarm exertion in spiritual practice is a great danger. And here, too, Sri Ramakrishna would employ his pithy, imperative sentence, "Dive deep."

Once a devotee named Ishan Chandra Mukherjee came to visit the Master at Dakshineswar. Sri Ramakrishna was fond of him and gave him spiritual instructions. On this occasion, after a little conversation with the Master, Ishan took his leave in order to perform the *sandhya* ritual in front of the Kali temple.[11] Later in the evening Sri Ramakrishna came upon him engaged in this act of devotion. In a rapturous mood he remarked, "What? ... Are you still performing the sandhya? ... How

---

[9] *Gospel,* pp. 475-76.

[10] *Gospel,* p. 465.

[11] The sandhya is a ritualistic worship performed by orthodox Hindus at dawn, midday, and sunset.—Ed.

long must a man continue the sandhya? As long as he has not developed love for the Lotus Feet of God."[12]

Then the Master sang two devotional songs in praise of Kali that emphasized cultivating genuine love for the Mother, rather than routine virtuous acts such as counting beads, charity, vows, and pilgrimages. Addressing Ishan again, the Master resumed with words that were stronger still and sounded like a mild reproach: "You cannot achieve anything by moving at such a slow pace. You need stern renunciation. Can you achieve anything by counting fifteen months as a year? You seem to have no strength, no grit. You are as mushy as flattened rice soaked in milk. Be up and doing! Gird your loins!"[13]

Ishan was a man of affluent circumstance. Since he wasn't entangled in his family's affairs, he would often engage himself in self-chosen public activities. Sri Ramakrishna knew this and wouldn't let the issue rest. In the same mood of chastisement he continued: "What are these things you busy yourself with— this arbitration and leadership? . . . You have been doing this kind of work for a long time. Let those who care for such things do them. Now devote your mind more to the Lotus Feet of God."[14]

Sri Ramakrishna's counsel reached its climax when he asked Ishan to become mad with love of God: "Let people know that Ishan has gone mad and cannot perform worldly duties any more. Then people will no longer come to you for leadership and arbitration."[15]

The truth of the Spirit is the closest thing to us, yet it may remain the farthest away if, out of perversity, we do not care to see it. Great teachers like Sri Ramakrishna feel it is their duty to cure us of this obduracy. Truly has Sri Krishna said in the Bhagavad Gita: "What is night to ordinary people is day to the sage, and what is day to the former is night to the latter."[16]

---

[12] *Gospel*, p. 611.

[13] *Gospel*, p. 612.

[14] *Gospel*, p. 613.

[15] *Gospel*, p. 615.

[16] 2. 69.

42   Spiritual values are as clear as daylight to seers of Truth. They cannot comprehend how we, the children of immortal bliss, can remain satisfied with a world-bound existence, forgetting our spiritual nature. Hence, out of compassion, these messengers of God move among us, inspiring us to realize the supreme goal of life. They speak clearly and powerfully; they have reached Truth beyond any possibility of doubt.

And all these spiritual values become evident when we hear Sri Ramakrishna say: "Dive deep."

Swami Vivekananda and the Emancipation of Religion

SWAMI VIVEKANANDA'S GREATNESS AS A religious teacher consisted as much in criticizing religion freely (but constructively), as in eloquently delineating its merits. He never refused to admit that evils have been perpetrated in the name of religion. True, religion has been a source of strength, hope, and peace to humanity, but it is an undeniable fact that, because of religion, millions of men and women have had to pass through unspeakable suffering. How the same force can manifest these contradictory elements is surely an enigma. Swami Vivekananda's exposition of religion offers a solution to this riddle.

Swami Vivekananda liked to define religion as a liberating force in the highest sense of the term. We are essentially free, and anything that obstructs this freedom will be challenged. Progress in civilization is only the story of our fight against, and victory over, various influences that limit our freedom. Science, art, literature, technology, and philosophy indicate our triumph over the limitations imposed upon the body and mind.

Religion, too, is no exception. Its essential characteristic is an urge for freedom. While this urge is also true of other human endeavors, the liberation sought by religion is more comprehensive than that which comes from other disciplines. This is because what impedes our freedom is a colossal force—maya, or ignorance. The goal of religion is to achieve complete emancipation: returning to that absolute independence of Spirit which is our birthright. Lesser disciplines are satisfied with lesser freedoms. Religion should have no quarrel with these disciplines because they, too, aspire to liberate us from bondage. They, however, stop halfway; religion alone can reach the ultimate freedom.

44   Yet the great liberating force of religion sometimes becomes an agent for narrowness and hatred. Like the sun hidden by clouds, religion then ceases to shed light and warmth upon humanity. Such religion no longer possesses the power to give its followers that great freedom which is supreme knowledge and love. When fettered by bigotry, religion deserves to be censured.

According to Swami Vivekananda, the emancipation of religion from bigotry and dogmatism is more important than blind enthusiasm for religion. The world already has too much fettered religion, with heaps of man-made sanctions, prohibitions, dogmas, and bigoted assertions. On the other hand, the world is in dire need of emancipated religion.

Let us not think that fettered religion is the result of primitive superstitions, mythological beliefs, and incomprehensible rituals. Vivekananda would have been the last person to condemn these, even though they are not the highest expressions of the religious urge. According to him, they are necessary steps in the evolution of religion and can be of great help to earnest religious seekers. We have no right to criticize them. We should be grateful to them, for throughout the centuries these superstitions, rituals, and myths have offered an easy way to comprehend supersensuous truth.

Atheists, animists, and idolaters are not the real danger to religion, but so-called enlightened people who claim to be religious. Their faith, however, is less in God than in their own concept of God. They contradict themselves by calling God great and compassionate while asking Him to curse and destroy those who do not conform to their dogmas. Their piety consists of the regimentation of certain formalities of worship; their worship is superficial and vociferous, rarely leading to tranquillity and an indrawn mind. Their love is anchored in narrowness, and the kingdom they seek to establish on earth is not of God, but of self-aggrandizing potentates, brandishing swords of authority and pomp. The mad man in Nietzsche's *The Joyful Wisdom* was probably right when he said: "I seek God. . . . Where is God gone? I mean to tell you! We have killed Him—you and I."

How can we free religion? Swami Vivekananda's suggestions can be briefly summarized: First, we have to place religion on a broad foundation. The highest function of religion is not to offer a reward for faith in dogma or to forgive punishment in return for obedience, but to lead us to that infinite freedom which is God. God is not limited by time, space, or the law of causation. He is changeless and eternal. "Before the mountains were brought forth, or ever thou hadst formed the earth and the world, even from everlasting to everlasting, thou art God."[1] The Upanishads declare: "God is truth and knowledge infinite."[2]

We say that God is great. But what are the implications of God's greatness? This greatness cannot be hampered by any kind of limitation. Yet how foolishly we try to put restrictions on God! We assert that God cannot be this or that. We love to think of God as the God of Israel, God of the Christians, God of the Hindus, and so on. We declare that God can incarnate on earth only once, and that His saving message is exhausted by a single sacred book. Let us remember the words of Vivekananda:

> Is God's book finished? Or is it still a continuous rev-
> elation going on? It is a marvelous book—these spiri-
> tual revelations of the world. The Bible, the Vedas,
> the Koran, and all other sacred books are but so
> many pages, and an infinite number of pages
> remains yet to be unfolded. I would leave it open for
> all of them. We stand in the present, but open our-
> selves to the infinite future. We take in all that has
> been in the past, enjoy the light of the present, and
> open every window of the heart for all that will
> come in the future. Salutation to all the prophets of
> the past, to all the great ones of the present, and to
> all that are to come in the future![3]

Religion should lead us to a God who is really great—
bhuma, in the language of the Upanishads. No human concept can claim to represent God completely; no word is adequate to describe Him fully. God's majesty surpasses everything we can

---

[1] Ps. 90.

[2] Taittiriya 2. 1. 1.

[3] *The Complete Works of Swami Vivekananda,* 8 vols. (Calcutta: Advaita Ashrama, 1976), 2: 374. [Hereafter cited as *CW,* followed by volume and page number.]

46 know or imagine. Yet God is manifested through millions of forms and ideas in endless creative movements. Not a single "point-event" in the universe can be dissociated from God. God is all. Anything that is, is in God. When such a God becomes the central pivot of religion, religion is bound to be broad. It respects all creeds, all scriptures, all forms of worship. Says Vivekananda:

> All narrow, limited, fighting ideas of religion have to go. All sect ideas and tribal or national ideas of religion must be given up. That each tribe or nation should have its own particular God and think that every other is wrong is a superstition that should belong to the past. . . . All that was good in the past must be preserved; and the doors must be kept open for future additions to the already existing store. . . . The Personal idea of God or the Impersonal, the Infinite, Moral Law, the Ideal Man— these all have to come under the definition of religion. And when religions have become thus broadened, their power for good will have increased a hundredfold.[4]

We are sometimes led to think that religious broadness means adherence to some fundamental metaphysical principles that are more or less common in most religions, rejecting those elements that are points of discord. In our zeal for interreligious amity we are prepared to shear religion of rituals, mythological beliefs, and many age-old practices which seem superstitious to us. Swami Vivekananda had some words of caution against this brand of broadness:

> You cannot make all conform to the same ideas: that is a fact, and I thank God that it is so. I am not against any sect. I am glad that sects exist, and I only wish they may go on multiplying more and more. . . . If we all thought alike, we would be like Egyptian mummies in a museum looking vacantly at

---

[4] *CW*, 2: 67-68.

one another's faces—no more than that! . . . When
religions are dead, there will be no more sects; it
will be the perfect peace and harmony of the grave.
But so long as mankind thinks, there will be sects.
Variation is the sign of life, and it must be there.[5]

My idea, therefore, is that all these religions are different forces in the economy of God, working for
the good of mankind; and that not one can become
dead, not one can be killed.[6]

Through high philosophy or low, through the most
exalted mythology or the grossest, through the most
refined ritualism or arrant fetishism, every sect,
every soul, every nation, every religion, consciously
or unconsciously, is struggling upward, towards
God; every vision of truth that man has, is a vision of
Him and of none else.[7]

In the first place I would ask mankind to recognize
this maxim, "Do not destroy." Iconoclastic reformers
do no good to the world. Break not, pull not anything down, but build. Help, if you can; if you cannot, fold your hands and stand by and see things go
on. . . . Secondly, take man where he stands, and
from there give him a lift.[8]

Swami Vivekananda strongly believed that religion must be
lived rather than discussed. Unfortunately, religious enthusiasm
is often directed toward theological discussions or mechanical
rituals. We fail to realize that religion is a tangible experience of
the Spirit. Religion has to be gained from day to day. And for
this, tremendous self-effort and earnestness are necessary. The
old man, enslaved by hundreds of passions and prejudices, must
die. The new man with a transparent heart has to be born. The
great transforming power of religion becomes manifest only

---

[5] CW, 2: 363-64.

[6] CW, 2: 366.

[7] CW, 2: 383.

[8] CW, 2: 384.

48 when one seriously takes it as a matter of daily practice. Swami Vivekananda said:

> Show by your lives that religion does not mean words, or names, or sects, but that it means spiritual realization. Only those can understand who have felt. Only those who have attained to spirituality can communicate it to others, can be great teachers of mankind. They alone are the powers of light.[9]

A religious person is one who actually feels the presence of God within his or her heart at all times. Then spiritual Reality is no longer a matter of conjecture; the aspirant's whole life is thoroughly permeated by that Reality. As a consequence, the aspirant's personality develops wonderful love, knowledge, and peace. To the aspirant the whole world appears to be radiating light and sweetness. No anger, selfishness, or hatred can abide in his or her heart. That is indeed the truest freedom promised by religion. Its other name is perfection.

Swami Vivekananda would passionately discuss what he called a scientific outlook on religion. Science is an exploration of some mystery of nature; religion is the endeavor to solve the ultimate mystery of life, the quest for supreme Truth. Religion can and must be scientifically undertaken. The discovery of our true nature as free Spirit is not a myth but the object of an effective search. Observation, experimentation, and verification should be its keynote, as with any other science.

As a science, religion is vitally linked with the well-being of humanity. It is wrong to say that religion is escapism or wish-fulfillment. When we can develop a positive attitude toward religion, we shall find that it is the highest manifestation of truth.

Swami Vivekananda spoke for emancipated religion:

> Truth is nobody's property; no race, no individual can lay any exclusive claim to it. Truth is the nature

---

[9] *CW,* 4: 187.

of all souls. . . . But it has to be made practical, to be made simple . . . so that it may penetrate every pore of human society, and become the property of the highest intellects and the commonest minds, of the man, woman, and child at the same time.[10]

No longer will religion remain a bundle of ideas or theories, nor an intellectual assent; it will enter into our very self.[11]

---

[10] *CW*, 2: 358.
[11] *CW*, 2: 396.

THE SUN AND THE MOON
IN SPIRITUAL LIFE

IN THE INDIAN SCRIPTURES, VARIOUS objects of nature have been used as symbols to help us understand the deeper facts of spiritual life.

The vast ocean is a symbol of God, for it seems endless. Waves are constantly rising and disappearing into the ocean; so also, in the infinite Reality that is God, everything in this universe appears and disappears. Just as the ocean is the source and support of the waves, God is the cause and substratum of all. Everything returns to that basic Reality. The ocean is therefore an apt symbol for God.

Similarly, the river is a symbol for humanity. Just as a river passes through many hills, valleys, and forests, and eventually flows into the sea, we have our origin in God and are moving toward Him. Our lives flow along—sometimes through joy, sometimes through suffering; sometimes easily, sometimes with difficulty—but our ultimate destination is God.

Other symbols are the tree, the sky, the bird. These and other objects of nature are employed in the Indian scriptures to help us understand God, ourselves, and this world. One such symbol is the forest: In a deep forest where there is no trail, we become confused. How can we find the path? When we do not understand the true purpose of our lives, we are indeed lost in a trackless wood. The forest therefore symbolizes life in ignorance.

In like manner, the sun has come to symbolize spiritual knowledge while the moon symbolizes devotion. The sun gives both the heat that occasionally scorches and the light that illumines all things. With the rising sun the shades of night vanish, allowing us to see and act. With the dawn of spiritual wisdom—

that is, the knowledge of God, the awareness of our true nature, and a spiritual understanding of this universe—our confusion disappears. Without this knowledge we live in darkness.

While we are ignorant we do not understand who we are; we do not understand our true goal; we do not understand from whence we came; we do not understand this ever-changing world and the constant flux of life. Nor do we understand God. We have heard that God created this universe and that He is the source of all that exists—but these are only words. Yet both the scriptures and those who have attained the knowledge of God tell us that it is possible to dispel life's bewilderment. When divine wisdom comes, we experience an inner transformation and our attitude toward life changes; our emotions, thoughts, and behavior patterns change.

The Upanishads say that we can escape everything, but we cannot escape God. When we know the real nature of God, we shall see that He is everywhere at all times—in our every breath and in our very existence. He is the true Reality, more fundamental than time and space. That Reality is Consciousness; without Consciousness there cannot be space, for when we think of space and time, the basis of that understanding must be Consciousness. There must be an awareness of space as well as an awareness of time, and that awareness comes from God. Just as the sun illumines all things, God as the Light of all lights illumines everything—the stars, the distant heavens, this world, and our bodies, minds, and senses.

On the surface it appears that each of us is a small individual composed of a body, a life-force, a mind, and an ego, but illumined seers tell us that this is not the whole story. According to the Vedanta scriptures, the Self is our basic reality. The Self exists neither in space nor in time; It shares the truth of God.

This comprehension does not come through mere reading or reasoning, but through deeper inquiry, discipline, and meditation. Such knowledge fulfills our lives. When spiritual wisdom arises, life becomes deeply meaningful. Each of us then begins to see the face of God everywhere; we realize that there is a spark of God within ourselves. In all human beings God resides in the heart as the divine Light. If we know this, what should our attitude be toward our fellow human beings? Can we hate

52 others? Can we kill others? Can we be unfair and exploit others? God exists in each of us as the central power—the power in our lives, our minds, and our senses. All power, all light, all wisdom and all joy come from God. The same God is everywhere—in all human beings, plants, and animals.

In addition to giving light, the sun also emits heat. Just as the intense heat of the sun scorches everything, spiritual knowledge has the power to sear. What does it burn? It immolates our evil desires, passions, and wrong attachments—things that hinder our spiritual progress. A verse from the Mundaka Upanishad says, "When knowledge of God comes, it burns all our karma."[1] Every one of us carries a bundle of karma and past desires from life to life.

Karma consists of our good and bad actions; each action leaves an effect, and that effect eventually bears fruit. Good karma gives us happiness and bad karma brings us suffering. We cannot escape karma. Karma explains some of the problems in life, and it also spares God our reproaches. Otherwise we complain: "How could this happen?" "How could God take away my child?" "I have prayed to God; I am His devotee. How could God do these things to me?"

We are confused about God's mercy and justice, but the theory of karma tells us that our happiness and pain are our own creations. If we are careful about our attitudes and actions, then life will become easier for us. The essence of the theory of karma is that we build our own future. Karma is the chain that binds us to daily life, and it forces us to travel from life to life. But our spiritual goal is to stop this ceaseless, meaningless transmigration. We must transcend karma. This can happen only when we realize our true Self, which is ever pure and ever free. The Self is never bound by karma; the sun of Self-knowledge burns up all karma.

In ancient India children were initiated into the sacred thread ceremony. The initiate was required to repeat a Vedic prayer every morning. That ancient prayer, directed to the sun as the symbol of God, is known as the *Gayatri* mantra. The substance of this mantra is:

[1] 2. 2. 8.

God is the light which illumines all the worlds.
He is the light of Consciousness.
He illumines all things.
May that Light of lights
Enter my heart and illumine my understanding.

The Gayatri prayer invokes the light of God to illumine our lives, the mind, senses, ego, and even the external world. Sunlight is physical light, but the light of God is spiritual light. When spiritual light dawns, everything is seen in a different way. All things, including one's own self, are seen from a spiritual viewpoint. And what does such insight achieve? It eradicates our ignorance and fears. It brings us true strength and peace.

In contrast to the sun of knowledge, the moon is a symbol of devotion, love of God. The heat and light of the sun are essential for life and action, but we also need the moon. What does moonlight do for us? It brings an atmosphere of peace, sweetness, and beauty; these also are needed in life. Devotion to God brings moonlight into our lives—that is, gentleness and love.

Love of God is a thousand times sweeter and more peaceful than worldly love, which operates under many limitations. Worldly love is directed solely to our families and friends, but love of God radiates far beyond this. Just as moonlight falls on Africa, India, America, and all countries, when love of God enters our hearts, our love extends to everyone. The whole world becomes our own. We understand that we have found our most Beloved—the true source of all love, and the eternal companion of our lives. The entire universe then appears to be His playground.

For a long period in our spiritual lives, spiritual knowledge and devotion are not the same. But great sages have said that eventually they coincide. When love reaches the apex, there is no difference between knowledge and devotion. But until that time, just as the sun and the moon have dissimilar functions and our reactions to them are different, in spiritual life, Self-knowledge and love of God have varying roles to play. Knowledge frees us from ignorance and enables us to find the spiritual unity in all things. On the other hand, when a spiritual seeker develops love for God, the world becomes a heaven. The devotee is no longer disturbed by the turmoil of life and is at peace with the world.

No one can live without love; everyone must have someone or something to love. When devotees adore their families, they understand that this love actually comes from God. When they love the trees, the moonlight, the ocean, the snows, they see all these as expressions of the infinite love that is God.

Though devotees increasingly feel the presence of God within their hearts, their love for God in no way obstructs their loves in this world. Knowing that God is the totality of all love, devotees adore their children more intensely than ever before, realizing that they are loving God within the child. Similarly, when devotees love flowers, they know that it is God's beauty that is reflected in the flowers; they love the songs of the birds for they are reflections of God's divine music. Thus, love of God pervades, enriches, and purifies our lives.

Devotion to God overcomes the selfishness and limitations of earthly love, transforming it into divine love. When this occurs, the world appears to be filled with love, joy, and peace. Such an experience can well be compared to moonlight. Just as when moonlight descends upon us and makes us feel calm, gentle, and sweet, love of God imparts tranquillity and compassion to all those around us. Moreover, when a devotee tangibly feels God's presence, he or she spontaneously thinks, "I am as rich as possible, for I have God. My beloved Lord is eternal and timeless; I also am timeless. From life to life He will be with me. This divine love is an eternal relationship." At all times we must carry the presence of God within our hearts through the regular practice of contemplation, prayer, and the repetition of the holy name. And while we must not be impatient, we must be determined. Once the goal is set, we must attain spiritual realization.

If we follow the path of knowledge, we try to think of ourselves as Spirit—one with the Infinite. God is the ultimate unity behind our small individualities. When we follow this path, the conviction slowly comes that all dualities are one—the duality of the world, the duality of this body, even the duality of God. Eventually these dualities all melt away, leaving only the One, the Indescribable. Vedanta scriptures say that the highest truth of God is actually inexpressible, beyond mind and speech. For those who wish to experience the supreme unity of Spirit in order to rise above their own small individualities, the path of Self-knowledge is the most appealing.

For others, the idea of loving God is more appealing. They think, "I do not seek the ultimate unity. I want to keep God separate from me. He is my beloved master, or father, or mother, or friend and companion." In the path of devotion the mind does not fear duality. The devotee knows that this is God's world. The devotee muses, "Why should this world not exist? My body is God's temple; why should this body not exist?" Duality, in the moonlight of devotion, becomes sweet. The world becomes sweet, as well as the devotee's actions and behavior. The path of devotion retains duality, since it retains the distinction between God and the devotee. Viewing the multiplicity of this world, the worshipper sees that it is God who performs this cosmic drama. Creation, preservation, and dissolution are all the play of God. The path of devotion thus enables one's mind to look upon this world in a mood of love and peace.

Some people practice both the path of knowledge and the path of devotion and can harmonize them. Sometimes the mind of a spiritual seeker rises to the level of supreme Unity in which the body, ego, trees, and mountains do not exist for they are all one Spirit. In this state the meditator cannot speak. Such is the indescribable experience of *advaita,* or nonduality. Emerging from this meditation, the aspirant is no longer distracted by maya; the Absolute has become the God of love and the follower of the path of knowledge then functions as a devotee of God, viewing this world in all its multiplicity, but remaining undisturbed. Now there is moonlight in his or her life. As a consequence the devotee says, "It is all God, my Beloved. The same infinite Unity manifests as the manifold universe." In a mood of devotion he or she may sing devotional songs to God. Indeed, it is entirely possible for the same devotee to experience both Self-knowledge and devotion to God. A fine blending and harmony can exist. Eventually there comes a time when the devotee's love becomes one with knowledge.

There is a Sufi story which says that once on a rainy evening a maiden was seated in her quiet abode. Her lover rapped on the door, but the portal did not open. Again his knock was heard, and the girl's voice inquired, "Who is there?" The visitor spoke his name, but the door remained secure. Then the youth implored, "I am your friend, your lover. Please unbar the door!" Even then he did not gain entry. At last he demanded, "Open the door! I am *yourself.*" And the door finally opened. His love had reached the level of identification in which he thought, "There is no difference between you and me." In the same way, the spiritual seeker comes to feel, "God is my Beloved, God is now one with me." Through knowledge the devotee attains the experience of unity; the same feeling of unity with God can come through devotion. Thus love and knowledge merge into one; this is seen in the lives of many saints. In the final analysis, there is no difference between knowledge and devotion.

Spiritual life truly brings fulfillment to human life. Through intellectual life, business life, physical life, we can satisfy various potentialities, yet spiritual life is the most significant achievement. We should make complete use of whatever gifts God has given us. But we should also remember, a spiritual gift is the most precious gift from God. To know God, love God, rise above ignorance, feel unity with all beings, and conquer death are spiritual desires, deeply ingrained in the human mind. God has given us all these in subtle form; it is for us to develop such potentialities.

EXPANSION
AND CONTRACTION

BEFORE EMBARKING ON A JOURNEY, a traveler collects various necessities from his or her home and then packs them securely in a suitcase. Once the traveler reaches the destination, those articles are removed and put in different places throughout the new location. The objects which were scattered were first collected and then spread out again. This is an example of contraction and expansion.

When we close our fists, our hands contract. When we open them to perform some action, our hands expand. Our daily lives are filled with similar examples of the twofold process of expansion and contraction. If we are observant, we can see the process occurring on many levels: physical, chemical, biological, financial—and even intellectual, moral, and spiritual.

We wake up in the morning to an expanded world—the sky above, the meadows and hills, the trees and the chirping birds. We gradually become aware of the noise of life with all its activities. The day ends, and at night we go to sleep. In sleep, the experience of the manifold contracts to unity. With the advent of the day, we again become keenly aware of an expanded world with all of our struggles before us.

We live in a world of endless multiplicity in both the waking and dream states. The converse of this occurs naturally in dreamless sleep. In sleep the external world of space and time and our mental world of thoughts and emotions disappear. Then again, we wake up to expansion and the cycle continues: expansion and contraction. This is the plan of nature.

58

There is currently a great deal of research into the nature of the universe; we are witnessing wonderful discoveries. Science tells us that this universe can be reduced to increasingly finer elements which can ultimately be reduced to energy. The universe eventually contracts into a tremendous ball of fire; the ball of fire bursts, and then the universe issues forth again. Thus the cyclic processes of the universe go on continually, for expansion and contraction are facets of nature.

Everyone in this life must endure suffering and frustration. Death is the inevitable end. No one can escape this rotation. When we think of this, the questions arise: What is life? Why do I exist? Why must I undergo all these troubles when the culmination of life is the disappearance of everything? That is when we seriously begin to ask the question, Why?

This is the beginning of our spiritual search. The search is for meaning—not merely in the external world, but in our own lives as well. We eventually reach the point when the terrible shocks and contradictions of life lead us to ask deeper questions about its true meaning.

In ancient India there were thinkers who asked those deeper questions. Their answers were recorded in the Vedas, which contain the accumulated spiritual knowledge of the ancient *rishis,* seers of truth. The culmination of the Vedas, or Vedanta, was expressed by the rishis in the Upanishads. Those rishis declared that there was a self-existent, timeless, spiritual Reality behind expansion and contraction. This Reality is the totality of everything: it is the totality of space, time, matter, life, and mind.

Everything that we encounter is included in that Reality. The name given to that Reality by the ancient seers was "Brahman," which literally means "the Greatest." The Greatest includes everything. Everything is contained in Brahman: the material, the psychological, the moral, and the spiritual.

All creation comes from that ultimate Reality which is Brahman. As we read in the Mundaka Upanishad:

> As from a blazing fire thousands of sparks issue forth,
> so manifold beings arise from the Imperishable, and
> verily return to it again. [1]

---

[1] 2. 1.

The well-known proposition of Vedanta is: The effect is not different from the cause. Whatsoever emerges from any source shares the nature of that source. So it is with fire: everything that emerges from a fire contains a bit of that fire. Brahman is *Satchidananda*, Existence-Consciousness-Bliss absolute; thus, any segment of the created universe is in essence Satchidananda.

Expansion and contraction can be seen on the cosmic level. According to Vedanta cosmology, *akasha,* which is akin to the modern concept of the space-time continuum, first emerges in the process of creation. After akasha, air, fire, water, and earth appear with their various permutations and combinations. In this way, the process of evolution begins and multiplicity arises. Everything comes from Brahman and returns to Brahman.

Another analogy can be given: A tree springs from a seed, and from this tree's seed a plant grows. By a gradual process, the plant develops into a tree; the tree flowers and then fruits appear. With the passing of the seasons the fruits drop, the leaves fall, and the bare skeleton of the tree remains. But the cycle renews itself: From the seed the plant springs forth, and then the tree, the flowers, and the fruits. Again, the cycle begins anew.

Thus expansion and contraction are continually in motion, and we are a part of the process. We are sparks of that fire which is Brahman. We are a little bit of Satchidananda, and there are millions of other bits of Satchidananda. I am a bit of Satchidananda, and so is the little bird. The river is another bit of Satchidananda, and so is the ocean. Whether great or small, everything appears, rests, and disappears into Satchidananda.

Scientists have conducted elaborate research on the vast reaches of space. Whatever research they do is welcome, because as the Vedic sages have declared: Whatever we discover is within God. God surrounds everything. Nothing can escape His reality. All that exists, exists in Brahman. Everything that happens does so in Brahman.

We all play our part in this world, but if we can remember that everything happens in Brahman, then we begin to develop an inner calmness and a balance between the body-mind complex and the outside world. This balance comes from

60 within the depths of our being, from Brahman within ourselves. Though Brahman emits this vast universe like sparks
from a fire, He remains unaffected; Brahman is the spectator of
the show. He enjoys the play of the cosmic process of appearance, sustenance, and disappearance. All changes happen in
Him, but He does not change.

From the Upanishads we learn that God, who projects this
play, wants us to discover the secret of the game. This play,
which Vedanta calls maya, binds us, but by taking refuge in God
and seeking His help, we can escape maya. Then we shall attain
the perfection and freedom which are in God.

We are a combination of body, prana (the life-force), mind,
and ego. But all these elements of the personality are centered
in the God that is within us—the Atman. Upon this Atman, layer
upon layer of coverings have been added, and these coverings
have deluded us. We must pray to God to solve life's mystery, to
allow us to see His face, even while we are living in the body.
When we are able to do this with sincerity, life becomes a life
in God. Nothing disappears; our duties remain, and our external
lives appear the same. But everything has changed color. Our
lives have become God-centered. Even when sufferings come,
we are able to bear them patiently.

When we suffer, we will not complain: Why did this happen
to me? Why to me and not to my neighbor? When our lives
becomes centered in God, our hearts will become quiet. We
will develop a different kind of mind: our minds will become
surrendered to God.

Self-surrender gives tremendous peace and great joy. "Thy
will be done" was the principle that Jesus Christ taught, and to
the devotee, this idea gives courage and strength.

The Upanishads declare that life becomes meaningful only
when we understand life's mystery. The mystery of life is simple: God is the Cause and the Ruler of everything. The
Upanishads declare God to be all-knowing. God knows
everything in detail and in totality.[2] Nothing is beyond His
knowledge. If a leaf falls, God knows that it is falling. Whatever
wonder science may discover comes from God. Science cannot

---

[2] Mundaka Upanishad 2. 2. 7.

discover anything outside God, because God is in everything. If a great scientist discovers a law and wins the Nobel Prize, God smiles and thinks, "Well, it is my law! I knew it before you!"

Brahman directs the three processes of expansion, sustenance, and contraction. Yet their existence is but momentary; the speed of the change is so tremendous that we cannot comprehend it. Atomic scientists are only now beginning to understand these subtle matters. The atomic processes occur at such a rate of speed that the scale of time is beyond our comprehension. We cannot comprehend one billionth of a second; such a unit of time becomes a mere figure of mathematics. Our minds cannot conceive it. Nevertheless, just as these processes are scientifically true, equally true are the actions of God in the world's processes.

Though God is vast and encompasses everything, though God is almighty and all-knowing, He is also kind, full of love, and very sweet. A justice of the high court is a very powerful man, and everyone dreads his decrees. Those under his jurisdiction fear the judgment that he will impose. But when that same justice returns home, he becomes a sweet husband and loving father. In the same manner, the same powerful and majestic God is—to a devotee of God—a sweet father, a sweet mother, a sweet friend, child, or lover.

The sages tell us that we can establish a human relationship with God. In our worship, prayer, and contemplation, we should follow the example of those holy people who have practiced the love of God through human relationships. These ideas and practices are known as *bhakti yoga*, or communion with God through devotion.

In the discipline of *raja yoga*, the aspirant collects the scattered mind and focuses it on the Atman—the divine Self within which is the immortal part of the personality. This yoga of concentration can lead a seeker to freedom from bondage.

Jnana yoga, the path of reflective analysis, is first a process of negation and then of affirmation. Initially the aspirant negates those things outside himself or herself, including the body, mind, and ego. The inquirer undertakes an inward journey, for just as there can be an outward journey into space, there can be an inward journey into inner space. The spiritual aspirant's goal is to find out who he or she really is. While there are different methods in the path of analysis, the object is the same: to eliminate all the distractions which obscure our ability to see the Self within. To do this we should retreat further and further from the layers of distinction, until finally the distinction between the object of contemplation and the one who contemplates is lost.

We need not be afraid to undertake this spiritual discipline because, as the great teachers and scriptures have declared, the inward journey reveals our real nature to us. We are only discovering our true identity. *Viveka,* discrimination between the unreal and the Real, and *vairagya,* dispassion, are the primary qualities necessary in the practice of jnana yoga.

Our true Self is the Self of everything. It is the Self of the sky and of the mountains. Everything that we see and experience has a core, and that core is this spiritual Reality.

At the stage of worship and prayer this Reality is an external God, but as spiritual life deepens, we find that the Atman, the Supreme Spirit, is infinite and has no limitations. We then find that our real nature is the same as the highest truth of God.

The majesty of Brahman is so great that words cannot describe Him, and the mind cannot conceive of Him. The Atman, the Self within us, is identical with That. This Atman is timeless; it is the source of all joy.

When we realize the Self, we will see the Self in everything. We will find ourselves in the sky, in the ocean, and in millions of other human beings. We will also find that the entire universe is within ourselves in the inmost core of our being.

The inmost core of our being is ever free. If we are serious and follow the precepts revealed to us by the sages, then we shall be able to find this perfection for ourselves. We will see that the multiplicity of the universe is an expansion of our own Self. Then we shall exclaim, "It is I who have become everything! It is I who have expanded; it is I who can bring the expansion into contraction; and it is I who am beyond both expansion and contraction." Expansion comes from within the Self, and contraction goes into the Self. When we understand this, the two words "expansion" and "contraction" are forgotten. We become speechless.

Sri Ramakrishna used to say, "A man cannot describe in words what he feels in samadhi. Coming down, he can give just a hint about it. I come down a hundred cubits, as it were, when I say 'Om' after samadhi." The terms "expansion" and "contraction" are good and useful analogies on the relative plane of existence. But in the spiritual world, this is a matter of realization, not an abstraction.

This may appear to be a very distant ideal, but we should nevertheless hear about it and think about it seriously. This is not an experience that we shall attain today or tomorrow. It is important, however, that we think about it and remember it, because that in itself will remove many of our attachments and prejudices.

When in the course of time we have understood and experienced the meaning of expansion and contraction, we shall not speak of creation, preservation, or dissolution. We shall be speechless, finding ourselves one with Brahman, forever and ever.

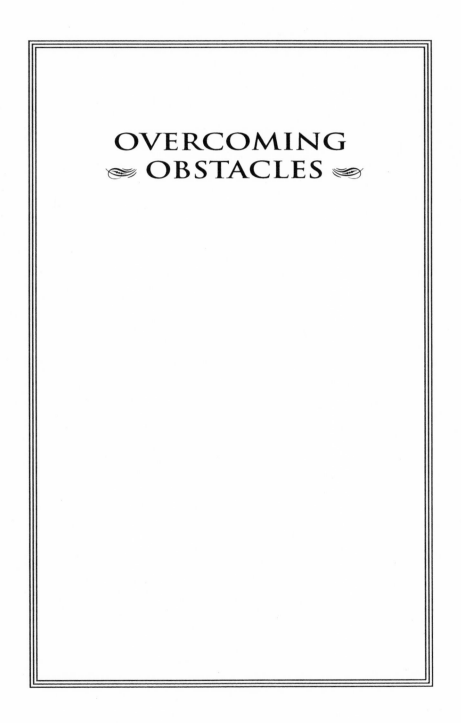

OVERCOMING
OBSTACLES

SPIRITUAL LIFE:
ITS CONDITIONS AND PITFALLS

> The subtle, extensive, ancient way has touched me. I
> have realized it myself. Through that the sages—the
> knowers of Brahman—also go to the heavenly sphere
> after the fall of the body, being freed even while living.[1]

THE "ANCIENT WAY"—A PATH extending from humanity to
God—cannot be compared to an American nonstop freeway.
This subtle, inner path has many stops and degrees of grada-
tion. In some areas it is level and smooth, and in other regions it
passes through difficult mud and gravel terrain. Its course may
run through the glaring stretches of a desert or along the sharp
curves and bends of precipitous mountains. In spite of all these
obstructions, we have to journey determinedly along this
ancient way leading to God.

Fortunately, there are rest stops all along the way which are
equipped with replenishing fuel, road maps, and guides. The
guides are experienced travelers who will give correct directions and assist in safe arrivals.

This ancient way of spirituality is lit with bright hopes, but
it also has dark pitfalls. It is a difficult but glorious road to
climb. Those who have succeeded encourage us to proceed
patiently and cautiously and warn us never to ignore the directions. They assert that we *can* reach the goal; we can *know* God
in this very life.

The highways and byways of ordinary life run in circles;
they seem to lead nowhere. When a seeking mind discovers
that worldly existence is only a treadmill and worldly pursuits
are futile, the flame of spiritual inquiry is ignited. The fear of
death, the promise of God, the intense desire to understand
love's deepest meaning, and a restless yearning for truth all
urge us to aspire to spiritual awakening.

---

[1] Brihadaranyaka Upanishad 4.4.8.

68

What is spiritual life? A life centered in God. It is not an unusual life. According to the attitudes we develop and the manner in which we live, our life on earth can be spiritual or nonspiritual. We are spiritual when the Divine enters our thoughts, actions, desires, emotions, and aspirations. Then He is not distant or theoretical, but a living God who guides our lives. The first pitfall, then, on the path to God is confusion about the meaning of spiritual life. Spiritual life is, in essence, to realize the divinity within us and to manifest it in our daily life.

A few basic requirements are necessary for effective and deep spiritual living. First we must have the faith that the goal we seek does, in fact, exist: There is a supreme, unchanging Truth—a Reality that is the foundation and the operative power of everything that exists. We have to believe that behind this world's flux, there is a cosmic intelligence, love, and unity that is God.

Though difficult to see at an early stage of the journey, it is necessary to believe that God can be experienced here and now. He is the supreme object of our love; He is our everlasting friend and companion. Somehow we must develop and strengthen this faith.

Let us take an example: Jesus Christ walked in the city of Jerusalem, teaching and consoling people and thereby changing their lives; it was in Jerusalem that the final scenes of his life were enacted. Faithful Christians everywhere hope to visit the Holy Land, but even though they may not have seen it, they never deny its existence. They know that many people have been to Jerusalem. In the same way, as we walk the spiritual path, let us be confident that although God is not yet visible, He is only a short distance away. He *can* be experienced—as many fortunate men and women have found throughout the ages.

The nature of God is infinite. He manifests Himself in endless ways, therefore the manifestations of God are various. He is impersonal—without name or form—or personal—with name and form. He can become an *avatar,* a divine incarnation, like Rama, Krishna, Jesus Christ, and Buddha. One should not be dogmatic about God's nature. Let everyone have his or her own conception of God. The Upanishads tell us that Brahman is both *saguna*, with attributes; and *nirguna*, without attributes; we can experience God on both these levels.

The second pitfall is lack of faith. How do we acquire faith? Spiritual teachers reply, "Through holy company." We need to seek those who are living in direct communion with God. We can witness in their lives the proof of God's limitless knowledge and love. Our weak notions about God become enlivened by holy company.

Holy company also includes reading the scriptures from all religions; they are records of the direct spiritual experiences of holy men and women. When we read the Upanishads, the Bhagavad Gita, the Bible, the Koran, and the sacred books of all religions, we catch a glimpse of spiritual truths. They speak of the joy, peace, and strength of spiritual life. When we read these accounts in the scriptures, our faith grows.

Another kind of faith is also necessary: faith in ourselves. Swami Vivekananda said, "First develop faith in yourself, then faith in God will come." Doubt is a serious pitfall along the way, a great obstruction in spiritual life. It limits our capabilities; we have to do away with it.

An individual's mind, body, and energy have limitations, but power and knowledge can be developed. There are great potentialities deep within the recesses of the mind. We all possess a hidden insight, an intuition, by which we can rise to the spiritual level and eventually reach the ultimate destination of life, the realization of God. We should therefore always be careful that our faith, both objective and subjective, is being nurtured.

A living and loving interest in spiritual life is an essential requirement. A joyful, enthusiastic attitude while actively following the directions given by one's spiritual teacher is necessary to avoid the pitfalls along the way. A joyful, enthusiastic attitude also develops purity of character. Actually, the Self, the essential truth of our nature, is ever pure. It is a spark of the Divine. Until we realize that inner divinity, of course we make mistakes, but these mistakes indirectly help us in our search for God. We should never brood over them. A healthy attitude is to be cautious and to decide not to commit those errors again. As we grow purer, we are less likely to make mistakes and lose our

70

way, and less likely to fall into pitfalls. We develop an attitude of renunciation, and we increasingly feel the Lord's presence in our hearts and minds.

Renunciation is a spiritual attitude. It is not the abandonment of home, family, children, education, or job. Rather, renunciation is a joyful disregard for undesirable attachments for the sake of God. The heart will be made pure with the development of this attitude. As Jesus said, "Blessed are the pure in heart, for they shall see God."

People are normally very attached to their egos, and think, "I am such an important person." There is some pleasure in this egotistic feeling, but when we come to spiritual life we have to give up this false pleasure. If there is too much egotism, it will obstruct our spiritual journey. Since we cannot give up the ego altogether, it has to be spiritualized.

To achieve this, we must undertake various spiritual practices. The regular practice of meditation, prayer, *japam* (repetition of a name of God, or mantra), contemplation, and spiritual studies is extremely necessary. Only earnest seekers will succeed: there is no room for triviality here. Not following a regular routine of spiritual practice is a serious pitfall. The quality of our effort in these practices determines the nature and course of our progress. No one can succeed without practice and perseverance.

We should avoid the pitfall of despair and confusion by seeking guidance from experienced people. Their counsel, in addition to the holy scriptures, is our "road map." Every phase of life, practical and spiritual, requires guidance. So in order to proceed along the "highway" safely, it is wise to stop now and then and seek instructions from an experienced guide, rather than pushing on blindly. Too much pride in ourselves with an unwillingness to learn from others is a stumbling block.

Another pitfall is our impatience. After hearing or reading about the blessings of spiritual life we become eager to have those experiences immediately! We begin to practice a little meditation for a week or two; nothing remarkable happens, and we feel frustrated. Then doubt comes and we impatiently say, "Oh, let us try another method." This impatience is the wrong attitude and a treacherous pitfall. Sri Ramakrishna used to say that if you want to dig a well, you have to dig in one place, and you have to dig deeper and deeper in that one place. Upon receiving proper instructions from an experienced spiritual teacher, we should continue our spiritual practice with great care and persistence.

Our interest in spiritual life should be genuine and deep, not superficial or shallow. A superficial mind cannot consistently adhere to anything. A person may have a little spiritual experience and then think, "Well, that is enough." But such people only fool themselves.

Our spiritual pursuit cannot have sincerity and depth if we remain attached to sense pleasures. The mind will remain on the levels of tamas and rajas, leading it restlessly outward. Lack of self-control is another pitfall, and we should make a regular practice of watchfulness over the senses. With the calmness of sattva, the senses can be tamed and quieted by developing self-control.

Watchfulness can be achieved by stepping back from the senses and trying to separate ourselves from them. We can observe the senses reaching outward like tentacles extending in all directions, fastening themselves on this object or that, impelled by desire after desire, and then returning to the repository of the mind. Through an awareness of the movements of the mind, we can filter out nonspiritual thoughts and ideas before they strike and contaminate the mind. We can avoid pitfalls by observing what is approaching the mind through the senses.

Another spiritual pitfall is vain argumentation; that is, too much intellectualism. Spiritual life is not words; it is one's own personal experience. When we take a college course in religious philosophy, we seek information and reason out ideas necessary for writing an article or a book. But for our own personal spiritual experience, we do not need very much information or argumentation.

When these spiritual practices become an integral part of our lives, and when we have made noticeable progress, a particular pitfall must be avoided: the reappearance of that villain—

72 the vain ego! The vain ego will enter, take the platform, demand applause, and claim: "I am such a remarkable person! Everyone notices how special I am." We should be on the lookout for this kind of egotism.

These are some of the roadblocks that can be expected along the spiritual way. Let us be conscious that these pitfalls are there, but we need not be fearful. We have only to be cautious and prepared. If we have intense faith and are humble, sincere, and patient, we need not be afraid of any pitfall. The spiritual path is a sure path. It will lead us to our destination, God—even in this life.

BLESSED SUFFERING

A MOTHER-TO-BE BOLDLY bears the pain of childbirth because the pain is necessary for her to have her baby. A person tending to an ill relative or a beloved friend may have to forget both food and sleep, but he or she does not mind these privations. The scientist who spends months doing research in the Antarctic generally does not complain about the terrible austerities involved in the project.

Familiar examples such as these can be drawn from many situations in life. It is true that the natural human instinct is to avoid pain, but often we have to court suffering for the sake of our own happiness. "Blessed suffering" is not a contradiction in terms.

When we come to spiritual life, suffering has not merely to be endured, but often loved. For many saints and seers, great agony became the door to illumination. The Sankhya philosopher Ishwarakrishna was being neither dogmatic nor pessimistic when he formulated the precondition of spiritual search as suffering: "One turns to higher inquiry from the impact of the three sufferings of life." [1]

If we are always surrounded by pleasure, and have no occasion to experience poverty, starvation, infirmity, or bereavement, we will have little chance to seek the Eternal at the back of the transitory. The spark of renunciation was not ignited in Prince Siddhartha while he was a captive within the walls of royal luxury; it occurred only when he saw the shadows of human misery with his own eyes.

---

[1] *Sankhya Karika*, Verse 1. The "three sufferings" are : 1) *adhyatmika,* subjective suffering, the result of physical or mental illness; 2) *adhibhautika,* external suffering caused by other human beings or animals, i.e., being hit by a car or bitten by a snake; 3) *adhidaivika,* suffering that comes as a result of natural calamities such as earthquake, flood, fire, etc.—Ed.

"Blessed are they that mourn: for they shall be comforted," said Jesus Christ.[2] By "comfort," Christ must have meant the blessedness of the experience of God. The price for that experience is "mourning"—that is, bereavement, dishonor, illness, frustration, and other sorrows. Hunger and thirst are surely enemies to life. Yet they may be friends to the spiritual seeker who is aspiring after a truth that is above this life. "Blessed are they which do hunger and thirst after righteousness: for they shall be filled," Christ declared.[3]

Sex as part of the path of dharma, or righteousness, is a well-recognized value in our society. Sri Krishna says in the Bhagavad Gita, "I am the desire in all beings that is not contrary to dharma."[4] Yet at a higher stage in our spiritual life, uncompromising chastity becomes the rule. We read in the Gita, "to gain which goal they live the life of continence."[5] Complete continence, though not necessary in numerous vocations of life, is a must in a higher mystical life. Jesus Christ said, "For there are some eunuchs, which were so born from their mother's womb: and there are some eunuchs, which were made eunuchs of men: and there be eunuchs, which have made themselves eunuchs for the kingdom of heaven's sake. He that is able to receive it, let him receive it."[6]

The last sentence of this teaching is significant. Christ did not mean to force absolute celibacy on everyone; there are gradations in spiritual life. One who has sexual relations with his or her spouse can, of course, practice religion and may progress to a considerable extent. But higher spiritual experiences require the attenuation of body consciousness; this is impossible without the nervous system being freed from the impulses of sex. Therefore Christ said, "He that is able to receive it, let him receive it." In humanity's religious history, many men and women have voluntarily "made themselves eunuchs for the

---

[2] Mt. 5. 4.
[3] Mt. 5. 6.
[4] 7. 2.
[5] 8. 11.
[6] Mt. 19. 12.

kingdom of heaven's sake." They have been ridiculed and condemned by many, but they themselves have cheerfully passed through the trials of self-denial.

In his teachings to monks, Buddha repeatedly depicted the blessings of the "homeless state." Home—which to a worldly person is the cornerstone of happiness—has to be shunned by one who seeks the highest spiritual freedom. This reversal of values does not indicate a morbid state of mind. The person who seriously treads the path of renunciation does so with full knowledge of its implications—its uncertainties, dangers, and sufferings.

An ordinary person rarely learns anything from suffering. Hit by affliction, he or she moans and groans helplessly and then, forgetting all about it, tries to laugh and dance again once the period of agony is over. Such a person basically does nothing to prevent the recurrence of the suffering.

Spiritual seekers, on the other hand, draw great lessons from sorrow; for them it becomes a door to spiritual elevation. From bereavement and loss of fortune the conviction of life's evanescence matures. Estrangement from friends leads spiritual seekers to see the inherent contradictions of life—the face of maya. Failures and disease teach them humility. Insoluble crises give them resignation to God. Kunti, the mother of the Pandavas, prayed to Sri Krishna: "Give me suffering, O Lord, so that I shall not forget Thee." Humiliation helps the spiritual aspirant to develop patience and forgiveness. "O Tulasi," wrote the saint-poet Tulasidas in a couplet, "go where people do not praise you. That will keep your ego low and the remembrance of Rama will be effective." When spiritual aspirants' hopes are frustrated, their frustration becomes an occasion for them to practice withdrawing the mind from the external world.

The Bhagavad Gita prescribes contemplation of suffering as one of the spiritual disciplines for Self-knowledge—reflection on the evils of birth, death, old age, sickness, and pain.[7] By such contemplation, we learn to look at the complete picture of life. Normally we face the world with many prejudices and false

---

[7] 13. 8.

assumptions. Our experience is always selective. We tend to ignore what is frightening and unpleasant, embracing that which is bright and pleasant.

But isn't life a mixture of opposites? Doesn't death exist side by side with life, doesn't illness walk behind health, poverty lurk behind wealth, dishonor wait to pounce upon fame, enmity stalk friendship, and frustration challenge hope? Duality is in the very fabric of our existence. To deny this is self-delusion, and self-delusion is never conducive to peace of mind.

The spiritual seeker has to examine life in all its aspects without prejudice or fear. Then the mind develops balance and becomes prepared to see that which is above the inherent contradictions of life. During this unbiased examination of the world, the spiritual seeker undergoes mental suffering. Many presumptions have to be discarded, many false anticipations are shattered, many pleasant dreams are broken. Yet this suffering brings great strength, power of judgment, and calmness of temper. It gives the aspirant the ability to look through the superficial and touch that which is really stable.

Voluntary suffering for religious purposes may sometimes lapse into a morbid self-esteem. In that case, suffering as a spiritual practice defeats its purpose. Fasting, vigils, celibacy, and similar self-denials are never ends in themselves. Austerity made into a fad often feeds one's ego and becomes a stumbling block to higher spiritual experiences. A sincere spiritual aspirant should be very cautious about his or her motives.

When a person faces suffering with the right attitude and as a means to a higher end, he or she cannot be called pessimistic. The sane attitude to life is neither pessimistic nor unduly optimistic. Wisdom does not cower when misery frowns, nor does wisdom lose its balance when pleasure is at the door. The eternal, infinite, spiritual Reality that is at the back of the universe and the core of our being is above pain and pleasure and all the dualities of our experience. Spiritual aspirants try to keep their vision pointed toward this Reality, living their lives with as much detachment as possible.

Those who seek spiritual fulfillment develop the capacity to disregard suffering. This capacity grows from a tangible experience of inner joy and peace as a result of prayer and meditation. For spiritual aspirants, God is not an empty concept. As they continue their spiritual practices, God becomes more and more real to them. The experience of God compensates for all the physical and mental afflictions they have endured in their journey. "The Lord is my strength and song," sang Moses. And St. Teresa of Avila wrote in one of her poems:

> Possessing God
> Naught does one lack;
> Alone, God suffices.

Ramprasad, the great saint of Bengal, expressed a similar feeling of fullness in the last lines of one of his songs: "Pleasure and pain are now the same; a sea of bliss is rising from the heart."

Men and women, not necessarily religious, who have dedicated their lives to the service of humanity, have had to pass through tremendous suffering. Many of them bear their ordeals smilingly. Suffering for them is a part of their mission; it is blessed suffering. Great spiritual personalities, after passing through the trials of self-denial during their stage of spiritual practice, have to face suffering again in a different manner. Impelled by the compassion for all beings that invariably follows God-realization, these great souls plunge into the service of humanity. Even though they have risen above the dualities of this world of maya, these great souls choose to live and work here. They gladly face what it offers them—cruelty, hatred, animosities, persecution, and even death. Their suffering is often keen, but to them it is blessed suffering.

Swami Vivekananda's poem "Angels Unawares" gives us a fitting conclusion:

> Then sorrow came—and Wealth and Power went—
> And made him kinship find with all the human race
> In groans and tears, and though his friends would laugh,
> His lips would speak in grateful accents—
> "O Blessed Misery!"[8]

---

[8] *The Complete Works of Swami Vivekananda*, 8 vols. (Calcutta: Advaita Ashrama, 1976), 4: 386.

DYEING THE MIND

OUR MINDS CAN WELL BE compared to an artist's canvas. Some European philosophers have said that when we come to this world we bring a blank mind, a *tabula rasa*. But many other thinkers, including the systems of Indian thought, state that we do not bring a blank canvas with us when we are born. Instead, we bring with us a mind already painted with the impressions of previous lives. In childhood all these impressions are not yet shown, but as we grow older, these *samskaras*, or latent impressions, manifest themselves. Whatever the mind experiences through the senses, imagination, or emotions, makes an impression which colors the mind.

For example, consider our visual impressions. We continually receive countless impressions from the outside world through our eyes; whatever we see is bound to impress itself on the mind. Some of these impressions may not be colorfast; they come and go and we forget them. But some impressions remain, and we can recall them as memories.

The same holds true for our experience of sound, touch, taste, and smell. The canvas of the mind is extremely elastic. There is no limit to its expansion; stretching farther and farther, it can receive millions of impressions. Every day, every moment, these impressions, or samskaras, are being added to the mind's canvas.

The impressions of emotions are also stored in the mind. For instance, we might have visited a holy place many years ago where we felt inspired or experienced some profound spiritual emotion. The experience left an impression that added another daub to the mind's canvas. Unpleasant emotions can also be retained for a long time. Once we may have had an unhappy experience with someone, resulting in feelings of anger or hate. These feelings usually do not end at that moment; through memory they can easily reappear in the mind. We are thus continually adding more pictures to the mind's canvas.

When we come to spiritual life, it is necessary to re-dye our minds, blotting out past impressions. Just as when we buy a house painted in a color we do not like and have to paint the rooms according to our taste, we do a similar thing when we begin a serious spiritual life.

The undesirable colors of the mind have to be eliminated and new colors must be brought in. Samskaras of faith, devotion, discrimination, detachment, and other spiritual qualities have to be painted over their opposites. This is a difficult but not impossible task. With great care and relentless effort we must cultivate what Sri Krishna calls "divine attributes" and what Jesus Christ calls "treasures in heaven."

A spiritual seeker who follows the path of knowledge tries to experience the one Consciousness that includes everything; Consciousness is his or her true Self. The seeker knows that the Self is not the body or the mind; therefore he or she wants to remove all the pictures and paint from the mind's canvas without any compromise, rejecting whatever ideas, emotions, and desires that are in the mind. The seeker asserts: "These manifold impressions coming to my mind are not real. They are just appearances. Sight, sound, smell, emotions, and memories are all maya." By such negation, the spiritual seeker removes all colors from the mind and replaces them with just one picture in just one color—that of Satchidananda, indivisible Existence-Consciousness-Bliss absolute. For a knower of the Self, there is nothing else but that infinite Consciousness, outside or inside, the one self-evident Unity. If any mental pictures come after Self-realization, the seeker does not try to give them reality or an independent existence. Instead the seeker says, "Everything is the Self."

The technique of those who follow the path of devotion is comparatively easy and pleasant. Unlike those following the path of knowledge, devotees do not have to be ruthless with themselves. They accept all the mind's pictures, but try to put new color on them. They relate all impressions—past and present—to their beloved Lord, the source of all beauty and harmony.

80   A particular face may create a disturbance in your mind, but if you feel that God is shining in all faces, you will begin to see that all faces are really God's. If there is beauty, it is God's beauty; if there is ugliness, that is also God's manifestation, because God is the indwelling Spirit in every living being. A devotee of God sees mountains, valleys, rivers, plants, animals, and instantly relates them to their Maker. Anything that comes to the devotee's mind comes through the light of God, and that light re-dyes his or her mind. How sense experiences can be spiritualized is beautifully shown in the following poem written by a Christian devotee:

> I see his blood upon the rose,
> And in the stars the glory of his eyes,
> His body gleams amid eternal snows,
> His tears fall from the skies,
> All pathways by His feet are worn,
> His strong heart stirs the ever-beating sea,
> His crown of thorns is twined with every thorn,
> His cross is every tree.[1]

In the creative imagination of this poet, the whole universe reflects the story of Jesus Christ's life. Every artist needs creative imagination; one whose mind is very matter-of-fact cannot be an artist. In the same way, re-dyeing the mind requires great imagination. "I see his blood upon the rose": anyone can see that a particular rose is red, but this devotee associates the red color with Christ's blood. Whenever the devotee sees any red color, he or she thinks of the great sacrifice of Christ rather than looking upon it as a material object. "And in the stars the glory of his eyes": the devotee looks at the stars and is reminded of Christ's eyes, the glorious eyes that shed compassion, sweetness, and tranquillity. "His body gleams amidst eternal snows": seeing the snow, the devotee is reminded of the body of Christ. Christ's body was not an ordinary body; it was the body of a divine incarnation—pure and holy. "His tears fall from

---

[1] Joseph Mary Plunkett, "I See His Blood Upon the Rose," *Poems That Live Forever,* ed. Hazel Felleman (New York: Doubleday & Co., 1965), p. 331.

the sky": seeing raindrops fall, at once the poet says, "These are the tears of Jesus Christ." Through creative imagination the devotee has associated rain with the tears of Jesus Christ, the tears of compassion that fell when Christ's heart melted at the sight of suffering humanity. The poet continues: "All pathways by his feet are worn." Jesus walked through the Holy Land, and for this devotee, the whole world has become Christ's path.

Our creative imagination has the ability to envision such things. This poet is actually re-dyeing the mind with new spiritual ideas. Thus the devotee continues: "His strong heart stirs the ever-beating sea": when the devotee sees the sea and its waves, at once Christ comes into his or her mind, for the heart of Christ is not the weak heart of an ignorant human being. Christ's heart is like the ocean. Watching the ocean, the poet remembers the mighty emotions that arose in Christ's heart; the waves have become his holy emotions. The "crown of thorns" and the cross are symbols of Christ's suffering for humanity. To this devotee's mind, every thorny bush and tree recalls the last chapter of Christ's life.

All sense impressions can be re-dyed. Take the case of smell: likes and dislikes are associated with the experience of smelling. A devotee of God sits in a temple and smells the fragrance of flowers and incense. This fragrance remains as a memory. Whenever any pleasant fragrance comes, the fragrance is associated with worship. When the devotee works outside in the garden, the fragrance of flowers rouses spiritual emotions: the devotee feels that in the cosmic temple of God these flowers are already offered.

Sound impressions can similarly be spiritualized. A devotee who practices the holy name of God regards it as the word-form of God—the essence of all sounds. During contemplation the devotee may feel that all sounds have joined in the mantra. Through creative imagination the devotee develops the ability to spiritualize all sounds and words. No sound or word can distract the devotee because his or her whole heart becomes filled with the music of the holy name.

For a devotee of God, the samskara of taste takes a spiritual pattern. When eating *prasad*, food that has been offered to God, the devotee feels that there is no taste in the world that can compare with it. It fills the devotee's heart with a new kind of joy. The sense experience of taste remains, but it has been transformed by being associated with God. In this way all the impressions that come to the mind through our various senses can be spiritualized, and the canvas of the mind can thus be re-dyed.

Desire is the one great distraction in spiritual life. Endless unnecessary desires have been stored in our minds: "I want this; I want that." Spiritual teachers tell us that we have to get rid of desires. This, of course, is a difficult task. But a person who loves God does not say, "I will banish all desires; I will kill all desires." Instead the devotee says, "I will transform all desires; I will recolor my desires."

There can still be desire for beauty, there can still be desire for love, but a devotee of God transforms all these desires. Once a young man, disturbed by sexual desire, came to Sri Ramakrishna and asked the Master how he could control his desire. Sri Ramakrishna answered, "Why should you kill your desire? Just turn lust for women into love for God." Similarly, when our hearts want to be proud, this pride can also be re-dyed. Devotees of God are the proudest people in the world. Their pride is in God, the highest treasure.

When we read the lives of great seers and saints, we find that they have transformed their minds' natural tendencies into spiritual tendencies. Everything that has been stored in the mind can be repainted. The spiritual seeker has to set up a studio with all the spiritual colors and the wonderful brushes of creative imagination. The impressions of lust, greed, pride, jealousy, hate, and attachment have to be transformed into magnificent pictures of God's beauty, power, love, sweetness, and knowledge. As the devotee increasingly masters the art of spiritual dyeing, no undesirable impression or subconscious desire will be able to trouble or terrify him or her. All experiences of the world are placed in the studio of the devotee's heart as wondrous paintings—the devotee's own creations.

The material world then loses its gross material nature; it becomes a world shining with God's light and love. The Vedanta philosopher Vacaspati Misra saluted Brahman as the

Being whose smile is this vast universe. Similarly, devotees will no longer find any obstructive, ugly picture on their minds' canvas. Every picture is bright with the color and life of God.

The *jnani,* one who follows the path of knowledge, tries to reach the unity of supreme Consciousness by shutting off the senses. Through the practice of detachment, the jnani removes all the pictures from the mind, negating all limited images. With the aid of the creative imagination, only one impression remains in the mind—that of the boundless, infinite Satchidananda. When the jnani attains Self-realization, he or she will once again see the manifold, but now in another light. The realized soul sees everything as Brahman, that same unitary Consciousness.

In the end, the experience is the same no matter which path is followed. Devotees call that experience God, and the jnanis call it their true Self. Vedanta tells us that the goal of knowledge and the goal of devotion are the same. When true devotees of God reach the ultimate goal through faith and love, they experience the same ultimate spiritual Reality that the jnanis reach by negating the world of experience.

In spiritual life we cannot afford to have the mind's canvas painted with undesirable pictures. We have to re-dye that canvas. In other words, the ordinary mind—full of distractions, passions, and desires—has to be repainted until it becomes a pure mind. Jesus Christ said, "Blessed are the pure in heart, for they shall see God." As Sri Krishna says in the Bhagavad Gita, the mind is both a great friend and also a terrible enemy.[2] When the mind has been transformed and given new spiritual colors, it becomes our great teacher. That mind guides us at every step. It has acquired the power of discrimination and protects us from the thrusts of maya.

We should not be afraid of the great task of spiritually transforming our minds. Spiritual life is really a great adventure. It is arduous, but if we are able to work at it patiently, we shall find that the labor is infinitely rewarding.

---

[2] 6. 5.

THE EGO AND
THE SELF

THE EGO AND THE SELF stand at two opposite ends of our spiritual journey. Our inquiry begins with the ego and culminates in the realization of the Self.

Broadly speaking, the ego can be taken as that part of the mind which expresses individuality. It is the ego that gives us the sense of "I" and "mine." The ego is the mouthpiece of the personality. The total personality is, of course, a very complex thing; it is not easy to understand how deep its roots are. Various factors in the body and mind such as biological urges, glands and neural structures, emotions, and other elements are involved in the construction of the personality. But so far as its vehicle of expression—namely, the ego—is concerned, there is not much difficulty in understanding and grasping it. Every moment of our lives we are keenly conscious of ourselves as individuals. When we think or speak or do anything, we know that the ego, our I-sense, is present. Its role is very important in our everyday lives. As a rule, there cannot be any activity, mental or physical, any understanding, feeling, or desire, without the sense of individuality in the background. The ego is the master player of our present mental plane.

There are, of course, certain exceptional situations when the ego might not be involved. For example, when we are deeply engrossed in some artistic object or while listening to beautiful music, our I-sense becomes attenuated and may even disappear completely. In common language, we say that we were so absorbed that we forgot ourselves. This is also the case in certain types of religious experience where the devotee is so moved by divine love that the ego drops to its minimum level. There is a spontaneous forgetfulness of oneself as an individual. For the time being one feels merged in the object of spiritual adoration. Except in these special cases, we find that the ego is always present in daily life. The ego is the thread that pulls the different elements of the individuality together and gives it cohesion.

When the ego functions, it associates with a wide variety of objects. The ego, by itself, is a neutral entity. But this neutrality ends in the field of operation. The ego has to identify with something, or else it cannot express itself. For example, the ego has to identify itself with the body. Then I say "I am healthy," or "My height is six feet." When I say, "I am thinking," my ego has associated itself with the mind. When I say, "I am angry," the emotion of anger is the object of association.

The ego in action changes from moment to moment. This moment it is linked with a certain function of the body, and the next moment with a state of the mind or an external circumstance. There is no limit to the objects or ideas with which the ego can connect itself. When we speak of ethical or cultural life, the ego is also there. It has only changed its center of identification. It now associates itself with ethical qualities such as virtue, truth, and purity, or with some cultural values such as poetry, science, democracy, resulting in the corresponding assertions: "I am virtuous"; "I am truthful"; "I am pure"; "I am a poet"; "I am a scientist"; "I am a citizen," and so on.

In these various cases of identification the ego connects itself with a clear understanding, but there are some extraordinary instances where the identification is only implicit. The ego can identify itself with ideas that are vast and infinite, though it is not fully conscious of this fact. For example, we implicitly believe that we are not going to die. All our thoughts and actions betray the strong assumption that we shall always be here, that we are immortal. But this belief is not expressly recognized; it is subconsciously assumed. The ego is similarly occasionally confronted with feelings of boundless happiness, knowledge, or tranquillity. Though we lack the time or courage to deeply ponder our kinship with these spiritual qualities, there is nevertheless an implicit identification in the background of our consciousness which we cannot shake off.

Yet were we without this kind of cosmic ego identification, life here would be miserable. We could not survive if every moment we feared death and were conscious of suffering, limitation, and ignorance. Fortunately for us, there is occasionally a sort of unrecognized, implicit identification of the ego with the Infinite.

This identification, however, is not clear in ordinary consciousness because it is superficial. It does not go deeply enough into the personality. We do not care to discover the true foundations of the personality, although we often use the word. We do not fully know what the mind is. Human beings have deeper levels of existence than the personality and mind, though in daily life it is not necessary to analyze or understand them.

The implicit identification of the ego with the Eternal and Infinite points to a basic Reality behind the universe and behind the individual personality. Vedanta calls this Reality the Self. The Self is the core of the mind and personality. It is also the core of the external world we perceive. When we probe deeply enough, we and our universe become one. The Self is that Unity: we live and move in that Unity. We can never escape our own nature. We are generally satisfied with the superficial manifestations of our personalities, but there is always an unknown element of our existence upon which the ego occasionally stumbles. In some moments of our lives we feel its presence as immortality, as infinite calmness and beatitude, as vast, undefined knowledge. Just as in our daily life the ego is the "mouthpiece" of the personality—the instrument by which the personality can work and manifest itself—so also in the field of Self-inquiry the ego serves as a "pointer" to the true basis of the personality, the Self.

The first role of the ego is understood by everyone. The second role has to be recognized by analysis and discrimination; many people never have a clue that there is a vast Reality in the background of their lives. Perhaps these people have had no opportunity for introspection. For such people, the Self remains unrecognized and undiscovered, perhaps for many lives. The desire to look deeply into life depends on a person's temperament and accumulated psychophysical tendencies. For those who take the question of spiritual life seriously, that vast, immortal Being—the Ground of our Existence—cannot be allowed to remain unknown and undiscovered. The highest goal of spiritual life is to realize that ultimate Ground, to know that at all times we are one with all that exists.

We have to begin, of course, with the ego, but our goal is to go forward until the ego discovers the Self. The primary function of the ego is to identify itself with this and that. The ego cannot help it. We have to bear with the nature of our egos, but at the same time we have to train the ego so that its tendency of identification is directed to supersensuous ideas and ideals. It has to be taught to associate itself with God. The ego then learns to call itself the servant or the child of God.

The ego seeks relationships. It becomes restless if it is left alone. The object of spiritual training is to give the ego spiritual relationships. Sri Ramakrishna used to speak of two kinds of ego—the ripe and the unripe. The ego that says, "I am the child of God, I am the servant of God" is the ripe ego. The unripe ego is that which attaches itself to different ideas and objects of worldly enjoyment. It says, "I am beautiful"; "I am powerful"; "I am wealthy." These identifications may be necessary in every-day life, but in the context of the highest spiritual goal, these notions are barriers. When you say, "I am the body," you have covered your true Self with a veil. For that reason Sri Ramakrishna said that the point of spiritual practice is to gradu-ally transform the unripe ego into a ripe ego. When a person does some work, he or she may say, "I am doing this." This is an expression of the unripe ego. The same activity can be taken up by shifting the ego's outlook. The person can say, "This body which does the work is God's tool. God is the agent." St. Paul used to say, "I live; yet not I, but Christ liveth in me."[1] Now the ego has become transformed; it has become the ripe ego.

There cannot be Self-knowledge if the ego is left to its igno-rant ways, sometimes identifying itself with this and sometimes with that. Each identification becomes a link in a chain binding us to this relative existence, and thus the vision of our true nature remains far away. The ignorant ego has been compared

[1] Gal. 2. 20.

88

in Vedanta texts to a terrible poisonous serpent, and caution has been given to the spiritual aspirant to always be careful of this serpent.

When we say, "I myself have done this," we are using two terms. One is the "I," the ordinary ego. But what is the "self" in "myself"? Ordinarily we do not care to analyze why we use these two terms. We also say, "You yourself have told me this." Using the third person we say, "He himself had come there." What is the implication of the word "self" in these three usages? The Vedanta analysis says: The "I," the ego, has only one face. It can be manifest only in the first person. But "self" is common to all three persons. It has three faces. It is behind him and behind you and behind me. It is the unchanging, undeniable, immediately experienced, abiding Consciousness behind all personalities.

Our minds, our intellects, our lives, even our world, are ultimately rooted in the Self, in that eternal Truth, though we do not ordinarily know this. We sometimes have only an implicit intuition of it. When we consciously try to discover this Self, that implicit intuition becomes more and more vivid. We become more conscious of our spiritual nature and give up all false identifications. We have been ignorantly accustomed to say, "I am a man" or "I am a woman" or "I am Mr. So-and-so." In order to break that habit, we have to declare: "I am the servant of God"; "I am unlimited Consciousness"; "I am one with eternal life."

As our spiritual comprehension matures and as the experience of the Self becomes more explicit, we find that this experience has nothing to do with any kind of objective association. That is why in higher Vedanta practices the method often used is that of negation. Positive identification is necessary up to a certain stage of our spiritual life. After that, the ego has to be taught to forget its old habit of identification and instead to practice saying, "I am not this body. I am not this mind. I am not these five elements. I am not thought."

The ego has to be trained to dissociate itself from whatever ideas of attachment come into the mind. This is a very difficult task, but if we gradually train the ego through spiritual identification, the ego can then be detached enough to take up these negating practices. Do these negations lead to emptiness? No. They eventually lead to the discovery of the Self, which is beyond both affirmation and negation. Then the ego will discover that its true nature has always been in timeless Existence, Consciousness, and Bliss—the vast tranquillity and freedom that is the Self. Not for a single moment were we ever dissociated from That.

The experience of the Self is quite different from the experience of the ego. It does not have to take the form of "I am." For the sake of contemplation we have to use such language as "I am of the nature of eternal bliss, eternal knowledge," but in actual experience there is no question of "I." The actual experience cannot be described in the language of the ego. Why? Because the Self is not something that stands outside of myself; the Self is my true nature, the eternal subject of all experience. We cannot express the Self as an idea or in words, in the way that we can express a concept or describe an external object. This is why Vedanta says, "neti, neti"—not this, not this. The Self can never be known as I know an external object; the seeker *is* the Self. When the veil of ego identification has been removed, the seeker finds that the Self was always there. Though the ego can point to the Self, the Self is, in fact, revealed only by Its own nature, and that experience is unspeakable.

What happens when Self-knowledge comes? What is the gain? Self-knowledge is the highest conceivable perfection. A passage from the Chandogya Upanishad says that when a person realizes his or her true nature, that person finds that the Self is not confined within one single body. "The Self is in front and also behind, the Self is above as also below, the Self is in the south and also in the north, all that is the Self."[2] In other words, the person of Self-knowledge finds that the Self is the all-pervading Consciousness. It is everywhere. Wherever we may go, the Self is there. This means that the Self is the Substratum, the Ground, not only of the individual personality, but also of everything that we experience.

The Self is the center of the whole universe. It is the center of all individuals. All time is in the Self, all space is in the Self.

[2] 7. 25. 2.

90

Everything is in the Self. One who knows the Self goes beyond ignorance. Knowledge of the all-comprehensible Truth, the Self, gives a person the highest satisfaction. The passage from the Upanishads continues: "One who seeks this, reflects on this, and understands this delights in the Self, sports with the Self, rejoices in the Self, revels in the Self. That person's companionship and sovereignty are in the Self."[3]

When we were in the state of ignorance, the ego was a passionate seeker of company; now we are in a position to tell the ego: "You are a natural companion of the Infinite. You need not seek association anymore. All objects, all beings, are already one with you." The knower of the Self does not require any other joy. The realized soul becomes the greatest emperor in this universe because everything has become his or her own. Not even the head of a pin can be excluded from the sovereignty of the realized soul. There cannot be any possible desire that is not fulfilled for that person. This state is attained through Self-knowledge; this is the goal which the ego must attain—its ultimate destination.

---

[3] Ibid.

To Encounter
Karma

WE BEGIN ENCOUNTERING KARMA AS soon as we are born.[1]

Our whole life is ceaseless action—tiresome, but unavoidable. When we retire from the waking state, we go to the dream state where we encounter dream activities. There, too, we cannot escape karma. Even when we sleep there is karma.

The question arises: What propels karma—this ceaseless chain of action? The answer is desire. We read in the Chandogya Upanishad that creation began from God's desire to become many.[2] Of course there is a difference between God's desire and our desire. God prompts karma into action—manifested in the threefold processes of creation, preservation, and dissolution—but He is above this play; He remains always unaffected. But we become enmeshed in desire.

The mind continuously creates desires. Why do we involve ourselves with seemingly endless desires? Why aren't we satisfied even though we know that perhaps only one percent of our desires can be fulfilled? The metaphysical answer, according to Vedanta, is that our true nature is an all-comprehensive Reality. Our nature cannot remain satisfied with little. We want totality: the totality of knowledge, wealth, health, and happiness. We unconsciously crave that totality.

Vedanta says that when we consciously realize the true meaning of desire, we can then begin true spiritual life. Then we know that the satisfaction of desires cannot be effectively

---

[1] Karma is action—physical and mental—and the effect of action; every action produces some effect. Good actions produce good effects; bad actions, bad effects. Karma is the ceaseless chain of cause and effect operating in the universe. On an individual level, karma is the consequence of a person's actions in this and previous lives.—Ed.

[2] 6. 2.

achieved by pursuing little desires in a piecemeal and fragmented way. We must ask and understand what the totality is. That totality is God, or our true Self.

Our desires prove that we seek God all the time, but do not know it. Actually, it is the desire for God that impels us to seek what is not God. This contradiction comes from maya.

The total fulfillment of desires is possible only when we reach God and understand our spiritual nature. When we realize our divine nature, we will not ask for little things, just as a multimillionaire does not ask for a few coins. But we cannot instantaneously understand that impulse of God in us.

Since we are born as human beings, we cannot be free from desires. We have to act, and that very process involves us in karma. Since we cannot escape karma, we have to encounter karma as best we can.

The question is: How can we encounter karma in such a way that we can become free from it? Let us not think that we face only the desires of this lifetime: the Indian spiritual tradition teaches us that we are travelers from life to life. In each life we create numerous desires, and the actions performed as a result of these desires leave a reaction, a fruit. Briefly speaking, it is said that good actions, *dharma,* leave good reactions which will bring happiness; bad actions, *adharma,* leave negative reactions which will cause suffering.

How can we escape from the heavy burden of our stored karma from the past and present? For most of us the pattern of life remains superficial: sometimes we suffer, sometimes we achieve success, sometimes we are frustrated, sometimes we laugh, sometimes we cry. But for some of us, deeper questions come: What is the meaning of traveling from life to life? The great spiritual teachers tell us that in reality there is no meaning in traveling from life to life. But if we try to understand that there *is* something *beyond* transmigration, then we can stop our meaningless encounter with karma.

Spiritual knowledge is the discovery of God, the discovery of our own spiritual nature. It is the only meaningful objective in the endless round of traveling from life to life.

When we seek spiritual knowledge, we encounter karma in a different way. Karma is motivated by desire and directed toward an objective. The spiritual seeker's karma springs from the desire to know God.

Encountering karma in a spiritual way does not mean running away from life, but rather running toward our spiritual destiny. If we can experience God, we can find real peace. God is beyond this so-called life which is bound by the laws of time, space, and causation. Therefore, for a spiritual aspirant, encountering karma becomes the way to transcend karma.

There are three ways to encounter karma fruitfully. The first way, the Bhagavad Gita says, is to do everything in a spirit of detachment. We are born with desires, but we must learn to curtail them in order to attain freedom. Whatever we do must be done with great responsibility and care, and we must not be attached to the results of our actions.

If we look into ourselves, we shall see that whenever we do something, we spend more energy thinking about the results than in doing what has to be done. We create dreams: "I will do this, and it will bring this result." Yet there is no certainty that these dreams will come true. The spiritual attitude is: A duty has come; I shall do it the way that it has to be done, but I shall not worry about it. When it is done, it is done; I shall take up another duty.

In this way, the mind undergoes great training, and we grow calm. The mind's restlessness is not really due to our actions, but to pondering their results. If we can stop that, we shall become ready for spiritual insight.

If we can encounter karma in a spirit of detachment, the first benefit we shall obtain is a sense of calmness. We shall begin to feel that although we are doing many things, there is nevertheless a feeling of freedom and peace in the background of our minds. This is one approach, and this can be effective even for a person who does not believe in God.

The second approach to encountering karma is to have faith in God. The Bhagavad Gita says that it is really God who moves all things. All the activities of the universe gain their power from God. If we can think that everything we do through the body, mind, and ego really comes from God, then karma becomes a spiritual practice. If you are a painter and have been able to produce a wonderful painting, as a devotee of God you will remember that it is by God's power that this wonderful work has been done. Whatever a faithful devotee of God does, he or she knows that it was done by God's grace and the result has also come by His grace. In this way devotees neutralize the bondage of karma.

Devotees are careful not to create unnecessary desires because they know that this world is not their permanent home. We are all traveling to God. If we can increasingly identify ourselves with our spiritual nature as sparks of the Divine—or as children of God—our identification with our little individualities will slowly vanish. Our journey will end by sharing the nature of God, and we will no longer be bound by karma.

The third way to encounter karma effectively is through knowledge. Those who follow this path are conscious of their own nature as the ever-free, pure Spirit. The Self is not really a fraction of the infinite Spirit, because Spirit cannot be fragmented. Our true Self is infinite and as such is eternally unattached.

Those who follow the path of knowledge try to feel that they are really the witness; in their contemplation, they separate their actions, senses, and the sense organs from their true nature. Their perspective is that they are unaffected by all the world's activities because they know that they are the Self. To be sure, those on the path of knowledge move, eat, dance, and do many things, but at all times they feel that their actions are part of a play to which they are the eternal witness. In the path of knowledge there is no question of God or offering the fruits of action to God; one encounters karma by separating oneself from *prakriti* through knowledge and the process of inquiry.[3] The way of knowledge neutralizes karma; those who follow it learn to separate themselves from karma by witnessing it.

Whatever method we follow to encounter karma spiritually, we must feel a love for our goal or there will not be much intensity in our spiritual practices. We are pilgrims on the way to God, and our journey ends only when we reach Him—just as a river emerges from some distant spring and ends its journey only when it meets the ocean.

---

[3] Prakriti is primal nature, the source of the universe. It is composed of the three gunas: sattva, rajas, and tamas. According to Vedanta philosophy, prakriti is a principle of maya and is therefore not fundamentally real.—Ed.

If we keep our spiritual perspective focused, the pattern of our lives will become different. A natural detachment and inwardness will result. The manifestations of ignorance—our pride, jealousy, intolerance, untruthfulness, and pettiness—will disappear ashamed, because our goal is God who is all peace and light, free and immortal.

For those who pursue the ultimate purpose of life, karma loosens its bonds and allows us to achieve what we have always sought—God.

THERE IS FEAR
FROM THE SECOND

THE GRAND MAXIM OF OUR spiritual struggle is: "There is fear from the second." The "second" refers to the idea of duality, our mistaken notion that something exists other than God. The quotation, "There is fear from the second," occurs in the Brihadaranyaka Upanishad and refers to the unitary experience—the supreme spiritual unity of everything.[1] This unity is our true Self; its nature is pure Consciousness. Finding this unity is the goal of spiritual endeavor. When a spiritual seeker moves toward this goal, any idea of duality becomes an obstruction and a matter of fear. The seeker's constant effort is to merge all objective experience into the infinite Self—the source and support of everything.

We have an innate urge for unity. If there is discord around us we cannot really function effectively, even in daily life. There must be a sense of unison, a harmonious cooperation, among the different elements of our lives. Take the case of the body. When the body is healthy, we feel it as a unity. There is no disharmony among the different functions. If, however, there is some trouble in some part of the body—the head, or the foot, or the stomach—that balance is lost. We feel that the unitary experience of our bodily well-being has been disturbed. If "seconds" in the form of aches, sores, and abnormal pressures assail the body, there is fear.

So also in the case of a happy family. The roof of the house is not leaking; there is perfect understanding between the husband and the wife; the children are well behaved, and there is a decent income. What is the subjective feeling of the family members? A feeling of unity. You feel as though you have

---

[1] 1. 4. 2.

extended yourself to the whole family—even to your house, the gardens, the furniture. There is nothing to disturb you; you are really peaceful. But, if some disturbance occurs in the family—for example, if a child becomes boisterous, refuses to go to school, and wants to be in bad company, then what happens? The peace of the entire household is disturbed. A "second" thing—namely, the disruptive behavior of the child—has intruded into your feeling of unity.

On a moonlit night we look at the sky. It is all so peaceful. Suddenly we see some alien object flying—not a bird, not a familiar passenger plane. Is it an aircraft from an enemy country, we wonder, or a spaceship from a different planet? Our peace of mind is disturbed. When we look at the sky in a mood of relaxation, we feel an experience of unity: we feel it is all peace in the heavens and in the stars. We extend the mind to the sky, and there is a feeling of unity. But if a second thing comes, a thing which we do not like, it disturbs our peace. In this way we are always afraid of things, people, and events that are foreign to the feeling of unity. From a philosophical viewpoint, the Upanishads call this source of disturbance "the second." Thus there is always "fear from the second," and that is what prevents us from experiencing the feeling of unity. When we come to spiritual life, this becomes a very important maxim. A spiritual aspirant seeks the experience of unity, which is God or our true Self.

The experience of unity does not come all at once; the seeker has to pass through various stages of development. For a long period of time the aspirant needs a God who is different from him or her; this is the path of devotion. In this path God is either an immanent God or an extracosmic God. In either case, God is separate from the worshipper. The seeker prays to God, meditates on Him, sings hymns to Him; for a long time these practices are necessary. We have to pass through the stages of prayer, contemplation, worship, self-surrender, and humility. But if we keep our hearts and minds open, then God will one day show His true face, the face of unity.

The highest experience of unity cannot be expressed in words or contemplated in an objective way. When we say, "God is my Father. He is the Origin and Creator of the world," we are making a dualistic statement. God is one and we are another. But when God, the world, and the individual become one, words can no longer describe that state because it is not an objective experience. It is a nondual experience.

God in his indescribable majesty is called *nirguna Brahman*—Brahman without any attributes. In the nondual experience, the individual reaches the highest truth. We exist in the infinite all the time, but we do not know it; it is a question of discovery. We must go deeper and deeper within to discover our own ultimate nature.

Before we are ready for Self-knowledge, we must go through the stages of dualism—worship, prayer, and spiritual disciplines. Much courage is required as well as great detachment. If we are attached to things, those things will pull our minds down. The mind also must be freed from all prejudice and dogma. Vedanta says that when the proper conditions are fulfilled, the nondual truth reveals itself. It does not descend from heaven.

When a person has a strong desire to realize the highest unity, the guiding dictum is: "There is fear from the second." The aspirant must apply this maxim sternly, without any hesitation, to all objective experience. Sometimes it may seem cruel. When the aspirant applies this principle to his or her own dear body, the aspirant must say, "Mr. Body, you are not me. I am leaving you, because you are a 'second.' I won't poison you, but I will burn you by the fire of knowledge." The seeker must constantly deny the reality of anything that is not the Self. This is the process of negation.

By negating the body and all objective experience, the aspirant does not go into a void. The Upanishads assure us that we are going to Brahman whose nature is fullness itself. The Full is so full that it cannot be described by words. The mind cannot comprehend it. If we insist on verbalizing or conceptualizing the true Self, we call it Satchidananda. But the Upanishads warn us that the highest truth of the Self is far above any positive description. Compared to the truth of the Self, everything else is a "second"—an obstruction. The spiritual aspirant uncompromisingly continues the process of negation, negating the body, mind, prana (the life-force), and ego; the aspirant negates the vast external universe and even its matrix, time-space. In the language of the Chandogya Upanishad, any objective experience is *alpam*, "little," and the Self alone is *bhuma*, "great."[2]

At a later stage in the process of negation, an "objective" God—a God whom we approach with mind and words—also becomes a "second." An incident in Sri Ramakrishna's life illustrates this point. When, under the direction of his guru, Totapuri, Sri Ramakrishna tried to merge his mind in the ultimate unity of the Self, one obstruction came. It was the image of the Divine Mother Kali. And for him that image was living; it was not stone. During Sri Ramakrishna's practice of negation, everything was easily negated—except his mind still beheld the smiling, living form of the Mother. The image would not leave his mind. He could not withdraw his mind from that divine form; it was too cruel. He tried and failed again, and his teacher became angry. Finding a tiny piece of glass on the ground, Totapuri picked it up and thrust it between the disciple's eyebrows. "Now concentrate here," he said. Accordingly, Sri Ramakrishna imagined that with the sword of knowledge he was severing the form of the Mother into two pieces. "Go, Mother, go!" he said. He found that the Divine Mother was disappearing. With a smile on her face she seemed to be saying, "You have passed the test. You are not really disposing of me; you are on the way to realizing my infinite truth."

The worship of an objective God also has to be negated because in the ultimate experience of nondualism, there is no room for "the second"—not even for a personal God. This is a stern discipline. But if a seeker can persistently follow it, he or she shall be rewarded—the true Self will manifest and the aspirant will experience the supreme Unity. The aspirant will find that this manifold universe in the past, present, and future is just an appearance.

The manifold is present in daily life in the waking, dreaming, and, in seed form, in the deep-sleep states of consciousness. It is even there in mystical experiences. But from the highest standpoint of truth, the manifold is not true. Only the indescribable truth of the Self is true; the manifold is nothing but a projection of the Self.

---

[2] 7. 24. 1.

100   The Upanishads prescribe intermediate disciplines to help us comprehend this unity. Anything that helps us to experience unity can be incorporated into our spiritual practice. The more individualistic, selfish, and isolated we are from others, the more anti-spiritual we are. Spiritual life is a life of unity and friendship. Anything that helps us to experience unity with objects and people, according to the Upanishads, will be helpful in realizing the supreme Unity.

Take the case of body consciousness. It is normally centered on my own individual body. But isn't it true that there is no difference between my body and the millions of other living bodies that operate by the same biological, chemical, and physical laws? There is unity among all these bodies. The Upanishads tell us to hold to this truth; it is not imaginary. Your body, his body, her body, millions of other living bodies—human bodies, dog bodies, cat bodies, mosquito bodies—all these bodies are nourished by Mother Earth. You are a piece of Mother Earth. That dog is another piece of Mother Earth. Spend some time in this cosmic meditation of unity. Your body is a part of this whole Mother Earth; your body, in reality, is cosmic. Your body is one with all bodies.

A stage comes when the seeker feels that the solid world is really a mental world. We cannot experience anything without the mind. The seeker feels that the body—apparently so solid and tangible—is really made up of mind and this manifold world is a world of ideas. Everything that is experienced becomes a particle of the mind. Finally, the seeker begins to understand the nature of Consciousness. He or she feels that all experiences are experiences of Consciousness, and the Self is the Ground of all Consciousness. The body, the prana, the mind, and even the external world are projections of the Self which is pure Consciousness. Space, time, matter, and energy are nothing but radiations of Consciousness that is the Self.

When this experience comes, there is no longer any "second" thing for the spiritual seeker. In deepest meditation, everything merges into that indescribable Reality. And when the aspirant comes back from samadhi, he or she sees everything as emanations of that great Light that is the Self. Seeing the Self

everywhere, the knower of the Self no longer behaves as 101
before. The knower of the Self feels unity with all beings. The
fire of knowledge burns everything that appears to be non-Self.
At peace with everything, the realized soul no longer experiences any duality.

UNDERSTANDING
THE MIND

INNER LIGHT

WHAT IS THE FUNCTION OF LIGHT? To reveal objects covered by darkness, and to illumine areas that are hidden. When we bring light into a dark room, we at once see everything in the room.

We often metaphorically assign light's function to mental and moral levels. We speak, for example, of the light of conscience. When the mind is troubled and cannot decide what is right or wrong, we say that a kind of darkness has blocked the mind. We need an inner light to show us the way. We call it conscience. Like light, it dispels the shadows of confusion and promotes clear action. Similarly, we could say that love is a light. When a person is lonely and has no one to care for him or her, life is really dark. But if someone appears who can understand and care for this person, the darkness disappears. Having new hope and joy, the world at once becomes meaningful with the light of love.

We could also speak of the light of compassion, the light of truth, the light of peace, and the light of knowledge. In each case a particular difficulty that can be compared to darkness is lifted and a positive experience of hope, joy, and fulfillment comes into being. These inner lights are more powerful than physical light. My world may be dark with regard to material possessions, yet my life may be shining in joy and peace because of the moral and spiritual light that has been kindled within me.

The most important inner light is the light of Consciousness. The Upanishads call it our true Self. It is the central light in the core of our being and it illumines all experience—including that of physical light. Even though we experience Consciousness all the time, it is very difficult to understand its real nature. Consciousness is the true essence of all existence. It has neither beginning nor end. It is eternal, infinite, and ever shining. What we call physical light—the light of the sun or of the moon, lightning's light, the light of the stars— all these lights are "illumined" (that is, these lights are known) by our inmost light—Consciousness.

Vedanta classifies normal experience into three levels of consciousness: waking, dreaming, and deep sleep. When we are awake, consciousness is always associated with some object—a sight, a sound, a smell, a thought, or an emotion. Anything we know—externally or internally—first has to be experienced through consciousness. When we look into the mind, we see a ceaseless stream of consciousness or "experience" in continual motion. We sometimes refer to it as objective consciousness since it is related to objects.

When we dream a similar thing happens, but in a different way: when we dream, there are links of knowledge and experience just as in the waking state; but when we come back to the waking state, we see that those experiences were not real. The most absurd things happened which we somehow accepted in dreams as real. But so long as the dream lasted, it seemed as true as the waking state.

Who is the dreamer? It cannot be the waking mind. How can the rational, waking mind, which knows the pros and cons of everything, be fooled by the incoherent occurrences of the dream state? It seems that when we go into the dream state, another mind is functioning, and that dream-mind is also rational—on the dream level. The dream-mind is a great creator and can add the appearance of reality to ideas. The ideas that emerge from the dream-mind are objective realities just as in the waking state.

In deep sleep there is also the light of Consciousness. Deep sleep is an experience of peace and tranquillity. We do not have objective experiences in sleep as we have in the waking or dream states. We not only forget our bodies when we dream, we also forget our worries, anxieties, duties, and responsibilities. This periodic forgetfulness of the waking identity is extremely necessary, not only for our bodies but for our minds as well. The mind's incessant movement—as we experience it in the waking and dream states—is a tiresome burden. We need relief from it. Sleep gives us relief; it is a pause from "knowing."

In sleep we completely forget everything. We are not conscious of the body, mind, ego, or of the past or the future or anything else. When we return to the waking state, we say to ourselves, "Oh, what a wonderful sleep I had! I wish I could have slept two hours longer!"

We do not scrutinize and analyze our sleep experiences deeply. In a naive way we say, "Oh, my sleep was so peaceful. I was so relaxed." We do not ask: What was this "I"? Was this the waking "I"? The waking "I" always needs an objective experience: sight, sound, smell, and so on. It is intensely busy. The dreaming "I" also needs either the "objects" of memories from waking, or those of its own creation. In deep sleep there is neither the waking "I" nor the dreaming "I." It is another phase of the personality. Recalling the sleep experience, we know that *we* did not vanish during that interval. In this phase of consciousness we had no objective knowledge as we do in the waking or dream states; there was an implicit awareness of self-existence and peace without the mediation of what we usually call the mind.

Vedanta advises spiritual seekers to coordinate and analyze these three experiences of waking, dreaming, and deep sleep, and from this, find out their real identity. A close examination of the three states gives us the insight that in the human personality there must be a common element in the waking, dreaming, and deep-sleep states.

This common element is the true perceiver of the experiences in these three states. In dream, a person does not remember the waking self; in deep sleep, both the waking and dream selves are obliterated. Yet we nevertheless feel an inexplicable continuity of identity throughout the three states.

This perceiver, the witness of the three states, is the inmost Light in us—the Light of eternal Consciousness. Vedanta scriptures repeatedly describe the glory of this Light, which is our true Self. The consciousness that we experience in our waking

108 and dream states, and even that which underlies our deep sleep, is a distorted, broken consciousness. Our true Self is pure Consciousness—Consciousness without an objective content. It is not bound by time or space or natural laws. It is the most fundamental Reality in this world or any other.

The sixth chapter of the Bhagavad Gita prescribes a basic way to find this inner Light. Through the practice of concentration, we have to withdraw the mind from distracting thoughts and direct it to the Atman—the shining Self within us.

A little faith is necessary, because in the beginning we have no idea how to reach this inner Light. But if we have patience, perseverance, and devotion to the ideal, the mind develops inwardness and transparency and slowly becomes able to touch the spiritual Reality within.

Self-knowledge can also be attained by reflective reasoning, or *vichara*. The Kena Upanishad begins with this question: "Who is it that enables the mind to think, the prana to function, the ears to hear, the eyes to see?" The answer is found by discriminating between the "seer" and the "seen"—the Changeless and the changing. The senses and the mind are in a constant state of motion, but the Self is the steady witness. Brain activity is possible only because of Consciousness, not vice versa. Consciousness is knowledge without any objective content. We are finally forced to see that all objective knowledge has its source in the Self—the inmost light of Consciousness.

In all periods of India's spiritual history there have been men and women who have discovered the truth of the Self. In the Brihadaranyaka Upanishad we read the experience of the sage Vamadeva: "It was I who have become the sun and Manu."[1] This "I" is not the waking "I" or the dreaming "I," but the true Self—the infinite Reality, eternal Consciousness, Existence, and Knowledge. Another sage proclaims in the Svetasvatara Upanishad:

---

[1] Manu is the progenitor of humanity as well as the ancient lawgiver; his code of conduct is the basis of Hindu social and religious law.—Ed.

> Hear, O ye children of immortality, even gods and
> angels, I have discovered my true Self, that ancient,
> infinite Being within my heart, that Light of all lights
> beyond all darkness. By finding Him, one can con-
> quer death. There is no other way.[2]

Immortality is not a theological concept. It is not a state
that we attain *after* death. It is a *truth* we can know here in this
very life. We have to find for ourselves that we are really timeless and deathless. As long as the mind remains in maya, ignorance, we seem to be in a world of phenomena with beginnings and endings. But when we have discovered the changeless Truth, death loses its terror. The eternal light of Consciousness is indeed immortality. Whatever is, is in the Self; the
Self is the totality of existence. The Taittiriya Upanishad says:

> When a person finds existence and unity in the
> Self . . . then only is fear transcended. So long as
> there is the least idea of separation from Him, there
> is fear.[3]

God is often described as light; He is the light of
Consciousness. Who but a God of light could have created this
universe of light? All created things are objects of knowledge;
they shine in Consciousness. Time, space, matter, energy, and life
are, according to Vedanta, forms of the fundamental Reality that
is Consciousness.

When we think of ourselves as material bodies, we are really small. We are constantly afraid of the impact of matter and
energy. Our bodies are just little clods of earth. How insignificant they are compared to the vast outer universe! Similarly,
when we look upon ourselves as psychological entities, we are
obsessed by a sense of littleness and fear. The individual mind
has very little capacity of understanding. It is always disturbed
by tensions and passions. Naturally we feel insignificant and

---

[2] 2. 5.
[3] 2. 7.

110 frustrated—how little we know compared to the vast accumulation of human knowledge! But when we see our true Self as all-embracing, pure Consciousness, the Light of all lights, our identity will then not limit itself to the body or the mind; we will become limitless. The world will not terrify us anymore. We will attain the source of all knowledge.

The function of light is to reveal: any portion of knowledge is really a kind of light. The mind has innumerable dark chambers; those who have never studied biology have a region of darkness in the mind as far as biology is concerned. If they study that subject, the chamber will become more or less illumined. The knowledge of astronomy can similarly become another illumined chamber. All the knowledge we acquire is a sort of progressive, yet nonetheless partial, illumination of the mind.

But Self-knowledge is total illumination. As the Mundaka Upanishad declares, by knowing the Self nothing remains unknown to us. When we have reached the inmost Light, we shall *know* that there is no more darkness anywhere.

Uplifting the Mind

ALTHOUGH NOBODY IS BORN PERFECT, everyone is equipped with a wonderful tool for progress, the mind. Because we normally do not understand the powers of our minds, we have to educate them. That is why we are sent to school where we learn different trades and skills. But formal or vocational education is not enough; we have to uplift the mind in other ways as well. One way is with moral education, which consists of training the character. If we have not educated the mind with moral values such as truthfulness, self-control, and humility, our lives can face disaster at any moment. Moral people are assets to themselves and to all those around them because they radiate strength, honesty, and peace. When we begin spiritual life, the mind requires another kind of upliftment—upliftment toward the Infinite.

According to the Indian spiritual tradition, the mind is constantly under the sway of the three gunas, the primary constituents of nature. The lowest, tamas, is the force of inertia, dullness, and stupidity. When the mind is alert, active, and ambitious, it is under the sway of rajas. Sattva, the third force, brings calmness, understanding, and happiness. It is possible through spiritual education to increase and develop the qualities of sattva.

The first quality of sattva is mental calmness in every activity. Consider Mahatma Gandhi. Here was a man who was tremendously active throughout his struggle for Indian independence. But a deep calmness was behind his every action. Such calmness can be found in many ways—through devotional music, contemplation, and meditation, for example.

Another sattvic quality is control of the senses. Our senses are like wild horses. As they receive and reject impressions, they react wildly and thus upset our mental balance. If we are upset, how can we receive the light of God? Therefore those who seek Self-knowledge and freedom must practice self-control. They must try to calm the senses through willpower. It is a great mistake to think that in order to enjoy happiness, our senses have to be wild. No. If a hungry man goes to a restaurant and wildly grabs his food like an animal, he does not really enjoy his food. But if he eats with calmness, he thoroughly appreciates the food he tastes.

Fearlessness is another quality that our minds must develop. We are always in fear of something. But since we are actually sparks of the Divine, we are entitled to divine attributes. Fearlessness is one such attribute. The more we experience God, the more fearless we become and the more we feel that we belong to God who is infinite power and freedom.

Another sattvic quality very important to our spiritual life is patience. Our general tendency is to do everything instantly. In every area of our lives we become restless and lose patience. If we want to drink coffee, we have to have instant coffee. We don't want to go to the trouble of reading a book; we want only short notes to help us pass an examination. We want an instant experience of God. But there is no instant samadhi. The great teachers tell us to patiently continue our contemplation, prayers, and disciplines, and not to expect immediate results.

Friendship is yet another quality that is important for training the mind. True friendship on the moral or practical level is one thing: I may be someone's friend, but if he or she stands against my interests, the friendship vanishes like a cloud. But spiritual friendship is different because it is based on a great spiritual truth—God, who is the golden thread of unity. As the Bhagavad Gita says, "All things are strung in me like jewels on a thread."[1] We have to try to feel this unity. The mind naturally wants to live in a little pond, but a spiritual person has to lift the mind and tell it: "You are acting like a little frog. You cannot live only in your little pond; you must live in the whole world.

---

[1] 7.7.

You must be broad-minded, for the whole world is God's."[2] In this way the mind increasingly experiences friendship with all of creation.

Closely related to friendship is forbearance. Great spiritual teachers have taught that if someone has done wrong, we must forgive him or her. Think of the story of the adulteress whom the Pharisees were about to stone when Jesus Christ said, "Let him who is without sin cast the first stone." Everyone was ashamed as Christ gently and compassionately told the woman to forget the past and begin leading a pure life.

Faith is another important spiritual quality. We are not born with a mountain of faith, but to achieve our goal in religion, we must have a little faith in God and in our spiritual potential. If I continuously think, "Oh, I have no hope, I am doomed to hell," then I become doomed to hell. But if I have faith, a flame is kindled within me. However weak that flame may be at first, it will grow. Faith comes through studying the scriptures and by association with holy people. Faith must be put into action; when idle, it does nothing, like gasoline stored in a can. But if you put the gasoline in an engine and a spark touches it, the gasoline does wonderful things. Similarly with faith: We have to think that God exists and listens to our prayers: He is within our hearts, and we can grow closer to Him through steady effort.

Then comes *bhakti,* or devotion. There is rarely a person who does not love something. A man may not love his wife or children, but he loves his fishing rod or his car. Unfortunately, our objects of love are constantly changing: I love a wife and

---

[2] Swami Shraddhananda is referring to the story of "The Frog in a Well," which Swami Vivekananda recounted at the 1893 Parliament of Religions in Chicago. A frog had been born and brought up inside a well and had lived there for a very long time. One day, another frog that lived in the sea came and fell into the well. When the well-frog asked the sea-frog whether the sea was as big as his well, the sea-frog was stunned to hear the ridiculous comparison. The well-frog nevertheless refused to believe that *anything* could be as big as his own little well. The frog in the well declared the frog from the sea to be a liar, and threw his visitor out. "That," said Swami Vivekananda, "has been the difficulty all the while." *Complete Works of Swami Vivekananda,* 8 vols. (Calcutta: Advaita Ashrama, 1976),1: 5.—Ed.

that wife may die after ten years of marriage; I marry a second time and that wife divorces me after one year; I marry a third time and that marriage does not work. Thus, our worldly loves are constantly frustrated. But if we raise the mind to the level of divine love, God—who is immortal and supremely beautiful—cannot leave us frustrated. The more we try to love Him, the more He responds. If we pray to God for a job or for money, sometimes He listens, sometimes not. But if we pray, "O God, I want to love you without any expectation," then God runs to us and says, "Yes, I am waiting for your love."

Yet another way to uplift the mind is to discover and rechannel its creative power. We use this power often in our daily lives. In spiritual life the same power has to be given an upward push so that the mind can discover its higher nature. Eventually the mind finds that Consciousness is its true basis; the scattered mind is just its external surface. The mind will increasingly come to feel that the mind itself is the source of all projections and that there is no end to its creative power. Eventually it discovers that this whole world is a creation of the mind—not the practical little mind, but the vast cosmic mind. Even if that experience lasts for only five minutes, that is a great achievement. When one returns to a normal state of consciousness, there is, in the back of the mind, the memory of that experience.

One way of comprehending this experience is to correlate our waking experience with that of dreaming. In the dream state there is a world like our own waking state. So long as the dream lasts, we know it is real, however absurd the dream may be. But who creates this dream? Vedanta says that it is the cosmic mind, since the little mind lacks such power. However, the cosmic mind buried in me can only be discovered by training and understanding.

The final stage is achieved when we go from the cosmic mind to the true Self. This ultimate level of upliftment is spiritual illumination. When we, through contemplation and meditation, discover our true Self, we find spiritual Reality at the back of all things. We then know, as Sri Ramakrishna declared, that the pure mind and the pure Self are one.

A spiritual seeker must be a great adventurer and probe 115
beyond the changing phenomena of life. The mind must not
stop at the level of the cosmic mind, but must continue on to
its own true nature, the infinite Self, which is beyond words,
thought, and individuality.

When the river reaches the ocean, it loses its identity and
becomes one with the ocean; so when we lose our individuality, we become one with the infinite Truth. This is what Vedanta
calls *moksha,* liberation—the highest freedom.

LEVELS
OF CONSCIOUSNESS

IF WE DESIGNATE CONSCIOUSNESS AS our foremost spiritual objective, our metaphysical inquiry is then very simple, because consciousness is a matter of familiar experience.

Western philosophers, psychologists, and physiologists have tried to examine and formulate the nature of consciousness from different viewpoints, and as a result, we have a wide variety of opinions about the origin and function of consciousness. Many of these theories oppose one another; a conclusion about consciousness acceptable to all seems a very remote possibility. However, on the following points these theories appear to have no disagreement. Consciousness

1. is a mental phenomenon intimately related to our brain and nervous system;
2. has no independent existence since birth, growth, and waking depend upon several factors: the sense organs, external stimuli, and the body's physiological functions;
3. is a sort of guiding light for the biological organism; it is essential for purposive behavior.

Contemporary thinkers seem to be more interested in how consciousness originates and functions than in what consciousness *is*. It is difficult for them to look upon consciousness as an entity independent of the object that one is conscious of.

We are always conscious of *something*—a flying bird, a wall, a sound, a touch, an odor, a thought or an emotion. According to many Western thinkers, objectless consciousness is an absurdity. We should not forget one important point:

When we study objective consciousness outside ourselves, we actually do not perceive consciousness as such, but the phenomena *associated* with consciousness. When we see a man showing his fist in anger, or a woman smiling in happiness, or an insect crawling in search of food, we are observing purposive phenomena. From these phenomena we infer that the man, the woman, and the insect are conscious beings. We never come into direct contact with their consciousness. Direct perception is possible only with regard to our *own* consciousness. To ourselves, consciousness is self-revealed. It is appropriate, then, that in the study of consciousness an important place is given to introspection.

An objective study of purposive behavior can never help us understand the nature of consciousness. It is probably not necessary for science to delve into the nature of consciousness by introspection. Science can remain satisfied with observing the phenomena of consciousness objectively, by external observation. But Western psychological science should not be dogmatic in asserting that the domain of consciousness extends thus far and no farther.

In fact, the sphere of consciousness is infinitely vast, and it can be studied on different levels. On each of these levels, our approach can be objective as well as subjective. The objective approach tells us what consciousness on a particular level *does*. The subjective approach is necessary to determine what consciousness on that level *is*.

If we are introspective and think about our own consciousness, we will observe that our own consciousness is like a territory where all our experiences take place. Just as all objects are in space and all events occur in time, so all experiences are associated with awareness. When we perceive anything, we are "aware" of it.

When we watch a thought or an emotion within ourselves, the process has to be accompanied by consciousness. When we are walking or playing, reading a book, listening to music, or making an experiment in the laboratory, consciousness must be present in the background of the mind. Even to perceive time and space, we first need consciousness. There is no thought unless we are conscious of it. We cannot speak of life if we

118 dissociate it from consciousness, for our very existence is a conscious existence. Consciousness surrounds us at every phase of life; we cannot approach a single point of the universe without our awareness. So long as we are awake, we cannot escape consciousness. Is it then unreasonable to view consciousness as fundamental a reality as time and space?

This all-embracing characteristic of consciousness can be understood only when we approach it through our own intuition. Viewed objectively in another subject—like a dog or a worm or even a human being—consciousness can be inferred as a unique quality of the biological organism, strictly limited within the organism, functioning under certain circumstances, and subsiding when its function is over. It has no more intrinsic value than hunger or thirst. In this objective view, there is no continuity of consciousness. It is strictly a psycho-biological phenomenon within the organism. It comes and goes with the impulse producing it.

However, when we approach consciousness through our own intuition, it no longer remains a matter of inference. We are in the midst of the radiance of our own awareness. There is no break in that awareness. Objects both internal (thoughts, emotions, feelings, etc.) and external (houses, gardens, people, animals, etc.) pass before that radiance in continuous succession and are instantly "known" to us. But that which links these objects with knowledge is the immutable Consciousness in us—vast, immeasurable, self-existent. It is the core of the personality. It is also the core of our experience. All existence rests in that Consciousness.

Though the true nature of Consciousness has to be grasped through our own intuition, it does not mean that each and every person will acquire such knowledge. It has to be developed by years of patient inquiry and discipline. The Katha Upanishad clearly states that what prevents us from realizing the ever-existent Self is our own foolishness: "One who has not first turned away from wickedness, who is not tranquil and subdued, and whose mind is not at peace cannot attain the Atman."[1]

---

[1] 1. 2. 24.

The true nature of Consciousness is always free. It has no birth or death. It undergoes no change under any circumstance. It is not bound by time, space, or laws of causality. It is the highest immortal Reality; it is Brahman. As conscious human beings, we always share that Reality.

Consciousness becomes "bound" when it enters into a subject-object relationship. Thus, all the knowledge and thought of our empirical life are manifestations of Consciousness in bondage.

Vedanta would say that this bondage is only apparent.

The true nature of Consciousness—Brahman—can never be blemished or undergo any change. The apparently transitory nature of Consciousness has to be ascribed to the mind with which it is associated. Thought-waves, or *vrittis*, come and go, but not the Consciousness which illumines them. In daily life, however, we cannot detect true Consciousness. As a rule we confuse Consciousness with the thought-waves of the mind, and as a result, we assume that Consciousness is transient, fragmentary, and variable. It is no wonder that some Western scientists equate Consciousness with vibrations in the brain.

Conversely, bound consciousness, characterized by a subject-object relationship, exists on many levels apart from our familiar waking experience. The dream state is one such example. In the dream state, we have a perfectly valid world with its manifold objects and occurrences in its own time-space-causality framework. Only when we wake do we realize the absurdities of the dreams.

In deep sleep we find another level of consciousness, which is quite different from either that of the waking or the dream state. The object in deep sleep is not from this manifold universe—as in the waking and dream states—but a unified mass of cognition. Sense experiences like sight, sound, and smell, and mental waves such as thoughts, emotions, and feelings have all conglomerated into a formless whole, without any specific content. This experience is bound to give us great peace, since the movement of the mind and senses has stopped. The peace of deep sleep should not be interpreted as a negative perception. Sleep is not unconsciousness from the point of view of the total human personality; it is unconsciousness in relation to the waking person.

120   In religious and mystical experiences, Consciousness functions on yet another level. In this state, achieved by prolonged practice of self-control and contemplation, the mind becomes so subtle and pure that when Consciousness is reflected there, the experience assumes the form of diverse, supersensuous perceptions. The form this perception takes depends upon one's spiritual approach. A devotee of Krishna may hear his divine flute; a devotee of Christ may see the beatific form of Jesus or Mary. A mystic who does not believe in the forms of God may experience peace and blessedness springing from the vivid revelation of an impersonal spiritual idea. While listening to religious music, an ardent devotee may have an ecstatic experience as the mind is lifted to an unusual level of calmness and joy.

Since these experiences imply a subject-object relationship (the subject is the devotee; the object, the forms and ideas of God), the experiencing consciousness still belongs to the category of the "bound." Spiritual visions have the power to transform our senses and mind remarkably; great calmness, purity, peace, and feelings of freedom, security, and joy invariably accompany these experiences. And yet Vedanta does not admit consciousness to have reached its highest level there. These experiences are significant stages on the path to the Highest.

The highest level of consciousness is reached when we realize it to be the eternal, infinite support of all experience, yet never attached to any objective content. This is the Atman, our true Self. The Atman is Brahman, the ultimate goal of our spiritual search.

Vedanta hesitates to use the word "reach" with respect to the Atman, since the Atman is always with us, our true nature. Never for a moment have we been separated from It. We are always That. The tragedy is that we have somehow forgotten our eternal heritage. This forgetfulness is called maya in Vedanta. All spiritual practices are for the purpose of removing maya—the basic ignorance of life—so that the ever-existent truth of the Self can be revealed to us.

Truly speaking, there are no "levels" in Consciousness. Its shining nature is retained under all conditions. What gives the idea of levels in Consciousness is the *upadhi*, the adjunct with which Consciousness is apparently linked.[2] Thus, we distinguish waking from dream, dream from sleep, mystical consciousness from empirical consciousness, and even in waking, we classify our experiences under various categories. However, from the standpoint of the Self, the essence of Consciousness remains unchanged in all these situations. It neither increases nor decreases; it is neither glorified nor debased. It is always pure, free, and immortal.

Supreme wisdom is to know that our conscious life is illumined at every moment by the Light of all lights, the Truth of all truths—our own Self. Rightly does the Kena Upanishad declare, "Brahman is known when It is realized in every state of mind; for by such knowledge one attains immortality."[3] And the Katha Upanishad says, "It is through the Atman that one knows form, taste, smell, sound, touch and carnal pleasures. Is there anything that remains unknown to the Atman?"[4]

The Consciousness which surrounds us at all times—inside and outside like time and space—is the highest Reality when we can understand its nature by freeing it from objective ideas which give it the appearance of transience. Consciousness is our own Self. All the epithets that describe Brahman, such as Being, Bliss, and Immortality, really belong to the same Reality.

The simplest way to approach this Reality is through our own consciousness.

---

[2] According to Vedanta philosophy, an upadhi is a limiting adjunct, a bondage of ignorance which the Atman imposes upon Itself by its identification with the body, mind, senses, intellect, and ego.—Ed.

[3] 2. 4.

[4] 2. 1. 3.

LIFE AND CONSCIOUSNESS

IN THE HINDU SCRIPTURES THE word "life" is denoted by both *prana*, which means the life-force, and *chaitanya*, or consciousness. Both life and consciousness are within everyone's daily experience. We feel that we are alive and that we are conscious. Nobody needs to point that out to us. Normally prana and chaitanya appear to be intertwined. In our daily life this does not matter. But great spiritual wisdom can emerge if we examine the two thoroughly and, if possible, separate them.

Prana is the internal principle of energy that keeps us alive. Anything that lives—whether human, animal, or plant—does so by the power of prana. Moreover, Indian philosophy extends the concept of prana to all other forms of energy in addition to the biological. Any kind of energy, such as heat, light, or electricity, comes within the scope of prana. However, for the present discussion, prana will be limited to the life-principle in living beings.

We know that breathing is the most conspicuous sign of life activity. If we were to stop breathing for even a few minutes, we would die. Air is therefore the most important contributing factor in the operation of prana. But there is another element in nature that is also essential for the sustenance of prana, and that is water. We know that we can go without food for many days, but we cannot live for long without water. The Chandogya Upanishad says, "Water pervades the life principle."[1]

Apart from breathing, prana functions in many other ways. Prana is the force behind blood circulation, digestion, and the body's other physiological processes. The prana is a unifying principle: the body's cells, blood circulation, digestive organs, heart, lungs, etc., all have their own distinct functions, but the

---

[1] 6. 5. 4.

unifying principle which coordinates these different elements is the prana. When this coordination is lost, we become sick; when there is perfect coordination, we are healthy. For example, if there is a wound in any part of the body, cells from the body's other areas rush there to repair the damage. Contemporary physiology has discovered many wonderful secrets of the prana principle working within us; it is a unifying, central power in the living body.

With a little attention we can feel the prana in the various parts of the body. If we watch the breath, we can feel the prana working in the lungs. We can feel the heartbeat, blood circulation, and nerve currents. The same prana works in all these physiological processes. The Vedanta and Yoga scriptures tell us that the prana's great power can be used in our spiritual evolution.

We are not just biological or psychological units: our lives have a spiritual frontier through which we can rise to our true, immortal nature. Spiritual life is the adventure of raising ourselves from our biological and psychological status to the spiritual level, and in this adventure, prana is a very important contributing factor. Prana need not remain at the biological level; it can be raised to a higher level by the techniques described in the Yoga and Vedanta scriptures.

Patanjali, the great teacher of Yoga philosophy, says, "Yoga is the suppression of mental waves."[2] The *chitta,* or mind, is continually producing vrittis, mental modifications. Once these vrittis are subdued, we can have a glimpse of the Self behind the mind.

There is an intimate connection between breathing and the mind. When the mind is concentrated, breathing is slow. When we look at a beautiful landscape with wonder, we feel that the breath has almost stopped. We use the expression "breathless": "It took my breath away," or "Listening to this makes me breathless." What does this mean? It means that the prana's movement through the breath has slowed; its energy has been transferred to the intense perception of the mind.

---

[2] Yoga Sutras 1. 2.

124   In yoga techniques, the practice of various kinds of regulated breathing, or *pranayama*, is accompanied by concentration on the prana energy. When we are excited, the breathing becomes rapid and the prana becomes excited. On the other hand, if the prana becomes slow and harmonious, the mind also becomes harmonious and calm. Through pranayama, the prana is prevented from working in its own biological way and is made to work in a controlled, subtle way.

The primary objective of pranayama is to attain mental calmness. But pranayama also brings about a transformation in the prana itself; it is raised from the biological level to a spiritual level.

Patanjali prescribes several practices for controlling the mind; one method is concentration. If, by the power of the will, the mind is focused upon a particular object like a deity, a holy word, or a pleasant material object, the distracting mental waves slowly subside and the comprehension of the spiritual Reality, the Atman, becomes easier. In any case, it is important that the mind remain controlled and harmonious. The mind then becomes calm and helps our spiritual practice.

The Upanishads prescribe the method of understanding prana on a deeper level. That understanding itself purifies and controls the prana very effectively. Purification of the prana means raising the prana to a level where it will cease to be biological—it will be a spiritual force. That can be done through some special meditations that are described in the Upanishads.

The starting point in these meditations is the analysis of prana. What is prana? We know the prana within our own bodies, but that prana also operates in other living bodies. The spiritual seeker therefore has to look upon the prana as a cosmic principle. The prana that is in me is also in other human beings as well as in animals, birds, and vegetation. This is not imagination; we can see it for ourselves by studying botany and zoology. These studies help us to understand the action of prana. Let us see how prana works, and then bring that observation into our contemplation. Let us contemplate the fact that the prana that operates in us is the same prana that moves in plants, animals, birds, and even microbes. By this meditation the mind becomes calm. Not only the mind, but the prana within us also becomes purified in the sense that it becomes universal and free.

In the Upanishads this cosmic prana has been given the status of a deity, and described under different names. Meditating on prana at the cosmic level has marvelous effects. Those who can think that the prana within themselves is one with cosmic life develop great serenity of mind; their outlook becomes very broad. Their attachment to this little life and their fear of death depart. They increasingly feel their identity with universal life. This brings love and compassion for other human beings and a spirit of fellowship with nature.

Understanding the limited prana in our individual psychophysical systems is also important for life's smooth functioning. Through the practice of pranayama, the prana energy can be made more powerful and harmonious. This in turn helps our physical organs to work better and aids in the prevention and cure of many ailments. Many people, particularly Westerners, are drawn to the practice of *asanas* (physical postures) and pranayama—not merely for the improvement of health, but also for enhancing beauty and longevity. But the effective practice of yoga needs other disciplines which many are not prepared to undertake. One is expected to live a clean, pure life. Truthfulness, noncovetousness, and chastity are the most important preliminary disciplines mentioned in the Yoga Sutras. When accompanied by these virtues, asanas and pranayama can certainly bring new dimensions to our physical and mental health. But we should not forget that the goal of yoga is to attain freedom—spiritual freedom—by knowing our true nature, the Self. Lesser goals, such as improving body and mind, should not be overemphasized.

When we see an ant crawling on the kitchen table in search of a grain of sugar, we understand it to be a unit of life. But we can also see the ant as a unit of consciousness because of its purposive behavior. In other words, that life unit is combined together with another principle, chaitanya, or consciousness. The same experience is true with regard to ourselves. When I am breathing, I am conscious of my breathing. I feel I am both a

126 living entity and a conscious being. Thus, in normal experiences, consciousness and life are combined together. And they may remain combined if we do not care for spiritual fulfillment. For biological and psychological life, it matters little if consciousness appears to be mixed with prana. But when we seek spiritual enlightenment, this mixing has to go.

Consciousness is a self-revealing experience. Nobody can see consciousness outside. Again, when I see an ant crawling toward a grain of sugar, I infer that there is consciousness in that ant. If I see a man sitting motionless against a tree, I wonder, Is this man dead? I go near and touch him. His body is there, but when I put my thumb under his nose I can detect no breath. When I push him there is no response. Then I say, "He is dead." Consciousness in others is not a direct experience—it is inference; but my consciousness is a direct, spontaneous experience for me. It does not need any other proof. Consciousness can be compared to light, because like light it reveals things. Through consciousness I know that this is my body; I know that it is four o'clock; I know that I am hungry or angry. In other words, whatever I experience needs the light of Consciousness for its revelation.

Prana has its limitations. The mind also has its limitations. But does Consciousness have limitations? Based on the experience of the seers and sages, Vedanta comes to the conclusion that Consciousness is completely separate from the prana and the mind. That is why we read in the Upanishads: "He is the life of life."[3] This means that Consciousness is more fundamental than the life-principle; it is more important than the psychological principle. "They who know the Life of life, the Eye of the eye, the Ear of the ear, the Mind of the mind, have realized the ancient Supreme Brahman."[4]

The ancient sages did not say that Consciousness arises from the brain. The brain is necessary as an instrument in the biological system to connect knowledge with action, and to coordinate all the different parts of the body. But brain activity should not be identified with Consciousness. When we look

[3] Kena Upanishad 1. 2.

[4] Brihadaranyaka Upanishad 4. 4. 18.

into our own knowledge of things, we have to separate Consciousness from the objects of knowledge. We do this by remaining an observer or witness.

Each of us in our own contemplation can try to watch our thoughts and heartbeat. If we continue this process, we shall see that this observation is very meaningful. This observation gradually gives us the conviction that the "I," the observer, is different from what is observed. In Vedanta philosophy this is called the analysis of the seer and the seen; in Sanskrit, *drg-drsya-viveka*. The observer is the conscious being in us known as the Self. The Self does not have the limitation of the body or the mind or the prana. The Upanishads tell us that the Self in us—the source of our consciousness—is an unchanging Reality; It does not depend upon anything else. Prana depends upon water and air; the body and mind depend upon food and many other things. But not the Consciousness within us. The Consciousness within us is a self-existent, timeless principle which has neither birth nor death.

After comprehending the nature of consciousness within ourselves as the silent, unchanging spectator in the drama of life, we slowly go to the next step. We have to know Consciousness on the cosmic level. We have to understand that there is only one Consciousness. "Those wise people who see that the consciousness within themselves is the same one Consciousness in all conscious beings, attain eternal peace."[5]

The Upanishads declare: "All this is the Self."[6] When we attain the highest knowledge, we see that our Self, the eternal Consciousness, is the total Reality, the supreme God. Whatever we experience—any fragment of the manifold universe—is nothing but a projection of Consciousness. The sun, the moon, the mountains, oceans, millions of living beings, prana, the mind—all these are projected from that eternal, fundamental Reality which is our true Self.

The highest truth about consciousness is that *whatever* we experience is Consciousness. We have to develop this understanding in spiritual life. From simple and ordinary experiences

[5] Katha Upanishad 2. 2. 13.

[6] Chandogya Upanishad 7. 25. 2.

128 we have to go to richer and higher experiences. And finally, when we realize that all experiences are parts of infinite Consciousness, we will reach the goal, the end of our spiritual journey.

The word "Vedanta" means "the end of spiritual knowledge." The highest knowledge is finding that ultimate unity in our own true Self.

THE INDIVIDUAL MIND
AND THE COSMIC MIND

A MAN AND A WOMAN were standing face to face outside the town hall, each of them trying to read the other's mind. The man was a professor and had just delivered a lengthy public lecture; the woman happened to be one of the audience. The professor thought, "She must be admiring my great scholarship." But as a matter of fact, the woman thought, "What a proud man he is! It is disgusting to listen to him." Clad in costly silk, the woman thought, "This gentleman must be captivated by my dress." What the professor actually thought was, "How vain of her to make a show of her apparel!"

Each person's attempt to read the other's mind was a failure, and that is what it should be. An individual's mind is an individual entity encased in a sort of impenetrable wall; it is extremely difficult for any other mind to have direct contact with it. Each of us has his or her own mind; it is not possible for our neighbors, even our closest friends, to know what is happening there. It is easy to have direct knowledge of another's body from its appearance, but this is not possible with the mind.

What we think we know of another's mind is often a conjecture. Confined within the limitations of our own understanding and unknown to others, the mind remains our most constant companion. It serves us in our physical actions, intellectual enterprises, and moral endeavors. Sometimes it is friendly. At other times it turns hostile. Even then we have no choice but to endure it. Finally, when we aspire to transcendental truth, it is with our own individual minds that we have to struggle. The mind must show us the way to go beyond the mind!

130

While the individual mind undergoes various degrees of transformation, both good and bad, the fact remains that at no stage is it possible for anyone outside of ourselves to experience it directly. Each person's individual mind is exclusively his or her own possession.

It is ordinarily not necessary to know the nature of the mind. It is enough for us to feel that we *have* a mind, and that we can receive its help in our various pursuits. But there are occasions when we wonder about its nature, and then we inquire about its constitution and modus operandi.

For example, I see something at a distance and my mind instantly has knowledge of that thing. Does my mind somehow go outside my body and touch that distant object? Certain schools of Indian philosophy explain perception with such an assumption. It is assumed that in perception, the sense organ (in this case the eyes) first contacts the object; then the mind—which is made up of very fine material—goes outside the body to form a wave, or vritti, which is similar to the object.

Again, when I am deeply engrossed in the thought of a dear person hundreds of miles away, I am totally oblivious of my present surroundings. Does my mind actually run to that place in some incomprehensible way? Similarly, when my mind is profoundly occupied in some past event and, for the time being, seems entirely cut off from the present, I wonder, Has the mind the magical power to move backwards and forwards in time? Yet another puzzle: I cannot put a hard and fast limit to the forms my mind assumes. This moment it thinks of a particle, the next moment, a mountain. The latter thought entails no additional labor to the mind even though its content is infinitely more "massive." The mind seems to have great liberty in generating thought forms.

These are some of the questions that we ask about our own minds. The professional psychologist may not bother with these naive questions, but sometimes sublime truths dawn upon us through simple channels.

Thus, when I am in a metaphysical mood, I may be led to attribute the following characteristics to my mind:

1. My mind is made up of very fine material—much finer than that of the body.
2. My mind has mobility. The ancient sages rightly called the mind the swiftest thing in the universe.
3. My mind is both extensive and pervasive.
4. My mind exhibits great creativity.

My mind is not rigidly confined within the walls of my body. It can act upon other minds. There may be an element of truth in the findings of clairvoyance and telepathy that cannot be summarily brushed aside—even though they speak of some unusual and incomprehensible phenomena. The Yoga philosophy speaks of many more interesting truths about the mind. The mind has unforeseen hidden powers, and by special methods it is possible to develop these powers and thereby extend the limits of the mind. Of course, to us the mind still remains an individual mind which operates through the body.

There are thus various gradations of the individual mind—beginning with the ordinary mind and terminating in the highly developed "yogic" mind. Different shades of intellectual and moral attainment lie between these two extremes. In none of these stages, however, has the mind ceased to be individual. But because of its inherent creative tendency, the mind sometimes rebels against the limitations of individuality. And that is how we are led to the concept of what is called the cosmic mind.

The notion of the cosmic mind is very old. It emerges from the concept of a personal God—God the Creator and supreme Lord of everything in this world. The personal God must be a conscious being. Since He is a conscious being, He must have a mind. However, His thoughts and mental processes are not similar to ours. At one single moment, He can apply himself to thousands of things! He can attend to some event on a distant star, and at the same time He knows what is happening inside the tiniest atom in our world. We believe that God has the power to know everything at every moment. Therefore God's mind must be a universal or cosmic mind. Whatever is, is in God's mind. Whatever happens is known to God's mind.

132

Even if we do not believe in God, there are other considerations that persuade us to accept the concept of a cosmic mind. We see order and creativity in this universe: where do they come from? When we look into our own minds, we find the ability to link diverse elements into a harmonious whole; we recognize and utilize cause-and-effect relationships between things and events. Ordered and purposeful thinking is a function of the mind; when we view the world outside ourselves, we see both an order in things and events that point to certain definite purposes. The universe is not chaotic: it is an ordered universe, designed and directed by the working of a mind. We must conclude that behind all these phenomena is a thinking mind. If we do not want to call it God, we can call it nature. But its essential function is to think in an orderly way, just as one's own individual mind thinks. And on these assumptions we know that many philosophers and some scientific thinkers—even apart from any religious consideration—have thought of this universe as manifested mind.

This picture of the cosmic mind can at most give us intellectual satisfaction. It does not give us the great spiritual satisfaction of comprehending our beloved God as the master Thinker and Creator, whose great mind operates throughout this manifold creation—that is the religious perspective. This religious perspective says that through prayer and meditation, our individual minds can come into contact with this great Mind in order to realize His knowledge, love, and joy.

When the little mind tires of its individuality, it tries to formulate a cosmic mind by means of logical reasoning. Through reasoning, however, the cosmic mind remains only a concept to the individual mind. It is a powerful and majestic thought, no doubt, yet it still does not have the unquestionable validity of direct experience. We cannot see for ourselves what the cosmic mind is. We can only *infer* the universal mind from certain facts within our own mind and certain facts outside ourselves in nature. Through reasoning, we cannot know what the cosmic mind is.

Vedanta has developed its own idea of a cosmic mind. According to Vedanta, the cosmic mind is not a mere concept, but an indubitable fact of our own experience. We can know the cosmic mind directly for ourselves. When I look into my mind in the waking state, I find it has two distinct aspects: first, the thought content, and second, the consciousness surrounding the thought. It is not possible to have a thought without being conscious of it. Thus consciousness operates throughout the mind, illuminating everything that takes place in the mental field.

"Thought" means conscious thought. It is a mixture of objective content and the intrinsic effulgence of the mind. As far as our waking life is concerned, we find that it consists of a series of "mixtures": sometimes a perception of sight, sometimes of sound, sometimes of touch, sometimes of emotions, desires, or feelings. These "mixtures" together have to pass through my mind, and every day of my waking life is the sum total of these separate mentations.

Then I go to sleep, and I dream. The waking life is shut off, and I am ushered into a new world. Many things not common to my familiar, waking world appear before me. I see people; I see things; I see events. It seems to be a new life, a new experience similar to the waking experience. When I wake up, I know that the dream world was purely imaginary—a figment of my mind. This is a common experience; yet the question remains how the mind can create, connect, and experience things in the dream state. Finally, why does the mind experience the dream-reality as strongly as that of the waking state?

While we dream, we do not realize that it is only the mind that is producing the dream. Only when we wake up do we discover this trick. Somehow the mind is able to create a world of its own with its own space and time and with its own notions of causality. The causal sequence in the dream is quite different from that in the waking state. Many strange things can happen which could not possibly happen in the waking state. The whole order of causality is topsy-turvy. The mind in the dream state somehow has the power to create things and to connect things so that even though impossible according to the rules of the waking world, they appear to be quite in order!

The experience of the dream state, when we thoroughly analyze its implications, forces these conclusions upon us: First, the mind in the dream state has unlimited power to create

134 things; second, it has the power to connect things in a new order of time, space, and causation; and finally, it has the power to lend a sense of reality to its creations.

Let us go now to another stage, that of deep sleep. In deep sleep I do not dream; there is no thought. But when I wake the next morning, I find myself refreshed. I think that I have slept very deeply. Temporarily at least, my nerves were soothed: I had no worries; I enjoyed great happiness. My memory gives me these ideas. The question remains, What happens to my mind and personality in deep sleep? My mind exhibits certain characteristics in the waking state; it exhibits other characteristics in the dream state. When deep sleep comes, what are the characteristics of the mind?

When I try to recall my experience in the deep-sleep state, I remember a kind of void; but at the same time, I cannot deny that I, as the experiencer of that void, was there. In fact, there is a feeling of identity in the different levels of experience. Somehow I retain my identity throughout these three states.

What gives me this strong sense of identity throughout these three states? Vedanta says that it is necessary to distinguish between the two aspects of the mind in the waking state: the aspect of thought content and the aspect of Consciousness. Thought and Consciousness are mingled in such a manner that we do not make a distinction between them; and for ordinary purposes it isn't necessary to separate the two. But when we come to the deeper truths of life, we must make a further analysis. There is a permanent element within the mind that gives us the sense of our identity throughout various states of experience; this is Consciousness. There is also a changing aspect of the mind that is the thought content. In Vedanta philosophy the first is called *drastri*, the knower, and the second is *drishya*, the known. The thought forms change, but the Illuminator of the thought forms does not.

From these clues, we can extend this knowledge into other directions to discover the permanent factor of the mind. Let us try to imagine where we were before we were born. A picture of darkness emerges and I say, "Well, I do not know. Perhaps it was darkness—suddenly I emerged. I was absent before my birth!" Superficially this seems to be a good answer. But if we analyze it deeply, we find that even with the concept of darkness or void, some element of my personality is convinced of its own existence. Somehow I, in a certain form, am standing in that distant past and am seeing for myself that void which existed before my birth. I can think of a void, but I am still there in some form. That is my sense of identity. In the core of my personality there is the same "I" even when I try to think of the state before my birth!

Let me now try to imagine what will happen at my death: One day I shall probably become ill; conditions will worsen, and gradually all mental functions will become dim. Then the heart will stop, and the body will die. I can visualize this picture, but what happens to that "I"? Unconsciously, I have not been able to withdraw my mind from that picture. In order to see my own death, I am present in some form in that distant future. When we analyze these concepts, the implications become clear.

It is not possible to annihilate the Observer, that element of the mind which continuously presents the sense of identity before us. Behind the series of thoughts of the ego—the "I" which is always present—there is an abiding element of my mind which is the steady Observer of things. The Observer of the waking, dreaming, and deep-sleep states, and the Observer of what existed before birth as well as after death, is the permanent factor of our minds that can never be eliminated.

Vedanta says that this permanent part—if we are permitted to use the word "part"—of our mind is Consciousness. Consciousness is something like a steady, unchanging light that throws its rays upon every thought; it is then that these thoughts become significant. Without this ray of light, no thought is possible, no experience is possible, no action is possible. The individual mind holds within itself a very precious treasure, the treasure of Consciousness. And this Consciousness is not an individual consciousness, in the sense that we speak of our individual minds. This Consciousness has no limit. Nothing can bind this Consciousness. All that we think of, and all that we come in contact with, is in the category of the second aspect of the mind, that of thought content—the *drishya*, or the objective element of the mind.

The conscious element of the mind is birthless and deathless. The individual mind always carries this great power, but we are not careful enough to see it. It is this conscious element that knows and gives our personality a sense of identity in and through all possible states of life. The purpose of Vedanta inquiry is to make us understand this aspect of the mind.

We can see that this permanent element of the mind, Consciousness, is nothing but the cosmic mind. If for a moment we can identify ourselves with this Consciousness, which is behind our world of experience—our bodies, thoughts, and actions—we shall know ourselves to be infinite, the Infinite Mind upon which all this manifold creation is manifested. Everything in this universe then becomes a thought of that cosmic mind which is Consciousness.

The moment I identify myself with that cosmic mind, I find that the whole universe is in me. This body, and whatever else exists in this world, rests in me. That is the declaration of Vedanta, and that is the real truth of the cosmic mind.

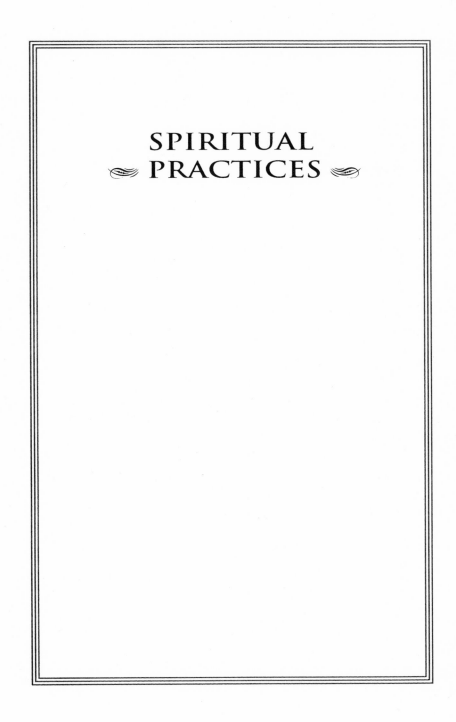

SPIRITUAL
PRACTICES

MEDITATION ON THE
DIVINE PRESENCE

THE GOAL OF SPIRITUAL LIFE is to feel the presence of God and to see the divine in all we encounter. One day this experience will come; we will feel the presence of God in the heavens, the oceans, the mountains, the flowers, and in all living beings—including ourselves, in our bodies, our minds, and our egos. We will feel the presence of God in all phenomena.

The Vedanta scriptures tell us that this is possible. While we live in ignorance, a wall hides God from us. Bit by bit, this wall has to be broken.

When we are leading a spiritual life, we need not calculate how far we have progressed. We need to practice the means by which the ultimate goal can be reached, and then—if we are patient and earnest—by God's grace we shall surely be able to feel the divine presence in all situations. Then the peace, knowledge, and joy that we seek shall come into our lives.

To experience the divine presence completely is a difficult task entailing the work of many years and perhaps many lives. But we must not give up hope. If we believe in reincarnation, we know that we have lived many past lives in ignorance. What does it matter, then, if three or four more lives are required? It is said that if we are sincere, we will not have long to wait. We should increase our spiritual efforts with hope, courage, and determination. Through divine grace, God-realization can come in *this* life.

Those who have realized God tell us that all we see and experience *is* God—Satchidananda, the immortal Reality, the light of pure Consciousness, and infinite Bliss. Most of us, however, cannot see God this way. This ever-changing world is so full of contradictions and suffering that it seems vastly different from God.

But spiritual experience is possible only through the mind's growth. When the mind is freed from desires and passions, we

140 will be able to understand what the divine presence is. We will begin to see that all is God, that it is God who is looking through all eyes, directing all egos, listening through all ears, thinking through all minds, and residing in all hearts. This is the experience of the divine presence. It does not evolve in one day, so we must not lose faith in the possibility of this vision. We have to begin our spiritual journey from where we are.

In the beginning, God appears extracosmic to us. We think that He is the Creator and Ruler, abiding in some distant heaven, managing everything by remote control. That philosophical position is called dualism. When we pursue such a philosophy, we do not care to inquire much about the nature of God. We take for granted that God is eternal, all-powerful, all-compassionate, and omniscient. In this dualistic attitude the devotee thinks, "God is different from me; I am bound, small, limited, mortal, and the world is ever-changing. But God is immortal, omniscient, free. He exists, and I am praying to Him to fulfill my life by granting me His vision."

With this dualistic attitude we can continue our prayer and meditation. If we persist, God will gradually begin to reveal His true nature. He will no longer seem to be a distant, extracosmic God. He will become an immanent God, the Soul of our souls, our very Self.

The Taittiriya Upanishad says, "Creating all things, He entered into everything."[1] The immanent God is thus present in every part of creation. God is not merely in one's own body, but in all human bodies. God is present as well in plants, animals, and in inanimate objects. Nature is not separate from Him. This philosophical position is called qualified monism in Indian philosophy. The One is qualified by the many; everything exists in God and is filled with God. This contemplation brings God as near to us as our own hearts, and our awareness of the divine presence is intensified.

Normally we look upon a mountain as a material mass of stone; this is the usual, ignorant outlook. Now let us bring a spiritual element into our contemplation: true, the outer

---

[1] 2. 6. 1.

appearance is a material mountain, but in the core of the mountain there is God.

In the language of the Upanishads, God is *Sat*—the infinite Reality. When the mountain is felt to be something actually existing, this existence is God. If we break the mountain into a million pieces, each piece will still exist. If we break the mountain into atoms, each atom still exists. Not a single fragment is without the presence of God as Sat, Existence.

This truth applies not only to the mountain, but to any other object in nature. Any material object is "material" on the surface, but metaphysically speaking, it is permeated through and through by God as Sat. Thinking of the mountain in the context of God as Existence can throw the mind into deep meditation. When the mind grows calm, the inner reality of the mountain becomes apparent, not only as Existence—Sat—but also as Consciousness—*Chit*—for Consciousness, or Knowledge, is involved in all existence. All that we experience comes to us as something that exists and shines as knowledge.

Finally, a third element has to be added, which may not have been clear to us in the beginning. This is *Ananda*, or Joy. In everything that exists there is the basic joy of God. Because we are ignorant, our experience of joy is selective. We find joy only in certain persons or events, not in everything. But we must enlarge our vision. We have to realize that Joy—like Existence and Knowledge—is inherent in everything and in every experience.

The mountain is a real object, but the source of that reality is God. The mountain is a unit of knowledge and that knowledge comes from God. The mountain is also a mass of joy and that joy comes from God.

It is through this perspective that we should look at nature. And to do this we have to alter our way of thinking. Normally our minds do not see God, but only the material form of the universe. In meditation the spiritual seeker's goal is to touch the core of Reality. This is not a poetical fancy. This goal has become the actual experience of sages who have beheld God and who have felt the divine presence everywhere. Following their experience, as we contemplate the mountain, the ocean, the forest, the sun, the moon, and all that we see around us, we

144 practice of meditation these ideas will become more real. We will increasingly be able to feel the presence of God internally and externally.

Even when we are working, our minds can be tinged with the divine presence. The spiritual seeker should know that God is the real doer. Our bodies and minds are His instruments. The Bhagavad Gita says: "By worshipping Him from whom all beings proceed and by whom the whole universe is pervaded—by worshipping Him through the performance of duty does one attain perfection."[4]

All actions proceed from God. In breathing, sleeping, eating—all things—the power for each action comes from God. If the devotee remembers this while working in the house, the office, or the shop, the ego becomes quiet and the devotee feels the presence of God.

As with everything, emotions also emanate from God. If an emotion of love for someone arises, the aspirant should recognize that it comes from God. The universal love of God is manifested in all our little loves for persons and things. Normally our love is tinged with selfishness, but if we can feel the divine presence in our human love, it will be a means for our liberation. A mother loves her child, but if she remembers that the sweetness, the beauty, and the charm of the child come from God, feeding and caressing the child become spiritual practices.

We have many opportunities to feel the presence of God in this world, but sometimes we forget this important truth. We think, "It is *my* child." Then if the child suddenly dies, we cry, "Where is my child? O God, why did you take away my child?" With the practice of the divine presence, we shall not suffer. Even if the child dies, we will say, "It is God's will. God brought me this child and made me love the child. It is all the play of God in order that I may find God."

If we are really earnest, we must find time to realize that it is God who operates the universe—that wherever there is beauty, wherever there is bliss, there is God. We must touch this Reality in our contemplation, and the memory of this will prevail in all the activities of our lives.

---

[4] 18. 46.

Spiritual life is a total life—a life that exists not only during meditation, but at all times. In whatever we do, God-consciousness can be there. Trying to feel the presence of God throughout the universe, knowing that God has penetrated every atom of this cosmos, brings us great strength, courage, and peace.

In Vedanta the final philosophic position for experiencing the divine presence is monism, the knowledge of unity. Nothing exists but God as Supreme Consciousness. In the dream state we realize upon waking that what seemed to be a solid, tangible universe was entirely created by the mind. Similarly, the waking world is a projection of Consciousness. The monistic vision allows us to see that the material world is nothing but Consciousness. Space, time, matter, energy, life, mind—all that we encounter and experience—are forms of Consciousness. It is all one Consciousness.

At this stage we try to concentrate on the ultimate Reality as Consciousness; we do not need to wander here and there to discover it. We discover it within our own hearts. We see the light of our own consciousness and know that this light of consciousness is one with the universal Consciousness that is God.

Then we try to concentrate on the universal Consciousness as our own true Self. Every experience that comes to us is at once merged into the universal Consciousness. If a thought of the body comes, we at once merge it into the source of all thoughts, which is the higher Self. Externally, the body appears to be made up of many components—bones, flesh, nerves, and so on—but it is all a projection of the Self. Slowly we realize that the entire universe, including space and time, is within ourselves. In this way the experience of the divine presence reaches its culmination; the true Self includes all things: the universe, the past, the present, the future, animate and inanimate objects, life and death. All these are one indefinable, indescribable unity—the unity of the universal Self.

We have varying degrees of comprehension of the divine presence. We must start from where we are and practice the divine presence as much as possible, knowing, in the language of the Chandogya Upanishad, that "All this is indeed Brahman."[5]

---

[5] 3. 14. 1.

Worship and Prayer

IN HINDUISM, WORSHIP AND PRAYER are two separate methods of communion with God.

Behind both of them is a common motive—love of God. The rule of love is to give something to the one we love, so it is natural for a devotee to want to offer something to God. This act is worship. Again, there are times when our love takes the form of wanting to ask something of the one we love; we feel that God loves us very dearly, and we are quite frank in making our needs known to Him. This asking is prayer. Both worship and prayer, far from being opposite in nature, are themselves expressions of love for God. They arise out of a common source that rests on three things: faith, love, and sincerity.

First, faith is necessary; we need the assurance that there is a loving God who accepts our worship or prayer. We need to feel that God responds to our expression of love, simple and humble though it may be, and lovingly accepts it; otherwise the worship or prayer merely becomes a mechanical routine, without meaning.

The second requirement is love. We need to approach God with an attitude of love, at the same time believing Him to be a loving Being—a loving father or loving mother or a loving master who does respond. If we believe that God is so wise, so sublime, and so majestic that we cannot reach Him, our worship and prayer will be hindered. Lastly, along with faith in God, and the belief that God is a loving God who will respond to our love, sincerity is required. Our worship and prayer should express the sincerity of our hearts.

Worship, as distinct from prayer, means giving something to God. In worship we do not so much seek from God as we are eager to express our love through offerings of flowers or fruit or food. We sing hymns of adoration to God. We must understand, of course, that worship does not appeal to all people. There may be spiritual development without an accompanying need for worship. A person of a highly metaphysical or philosophical temperament may consider worship to be extremely irrational behavior. The temperament that needs worship seeks an expression of love—not merely through contemplation, meditation, or prayer, but through a tangible human act of offering a gift to God.

Here the importance of sincerity must be stressed. If we sincerely love a friend, relative, or child, then reason or necessity counts for little—we simply *like* to give something to those we love. The same holds true in the spiritual realm; if we bring sincerity to our worship, our worship becomes fruitful, effective, and inspirational. Then as our spiritual realization deepens, the way in which we express our love for God also undergoes a transformation.

Just as our love in this world may not be completely without selfish motives, so in worship we may hope that, if we please God, He will fulfill some of our cherished desires or help us out of our difficulties. This motive-strewn type of worship is called *sakama*. And though it is not conducive to great spiritual progress, it nonetheless is permissible under certain circumstances and for certain types of people. For worship of God to be really a spiritual discipline, it should be based on an unselfish attitude, or *nishkama*, literally, "without desire." In this higher form of worship, we do not ask anything worldly from God. We only want God's love.

Why should it be necessary to show selfless love for God through external action? Sri Ramakrishna explained it in this way. Suppose, he said, a wealthy gentleman lives in the city, but owns a country estate miles away. There are orchards and flower gardens on the estate, and these he has placed in charge of a gardener. When on occasion the gardener goes to the city, he takes a basket of fruit or flowers with him and says to the master, "I have brought you these," as though they were from himself. Now the master knows who owns these things; at the same time, he appreciates the gesture of the servant who, out of eagerness, has come with the present, and he is pleased. In the same manner, whatever we offer God is already His; yet if we—His servants—bring Him some presents out of love, we can assume that He will be pleased.

This need for selfless worship by the devotee is also cited in the Bhagavad Gita where Sri Krishna says: "Whoever offers me a leaf, a flower, a fruit, or water with devotion, that I accept—the devout gift of the pure-minded."[1] Because He sees the inner feeling of the devotee, God accepts the external objects which merely symbolize the fullness of the devotee's love. God sees the inner heart, and He appreciates the devotee's sincere gesture.

Worship has different forms. Instead of being external, it can also be internal or mental, in which case the devotee imagines the ingredients of worship and mentally offers them to God. Again, the mentally conceived ingredients may not be physical objects like flowers or incense, but moral or spiritual qualities such as purity, forbearance, self-control, and compassion.

We should also remember that since God is the great purifier, even a selfish motive in worship may be a starting point for higher forms of spiritual realization. Association with God and remembrance of God absorb the worshipper's mind, and as he or she gradually becomes purified, the element of selfishness disappears from the aspirant's heart. This is how worship is transformed from worship with a motive to worship without a motive. After motiveless worship is attained, external worship is no longer necessary, as exemplified in Sri Ramakrishna's life. Sri Ramakrishna began his spiritual life with external worship. Then one day while preparing to pick flowers for worship, he suddenly saw that the flowers were already offered at the Lord's feet; these flowers were part of the continual worship taking place in this great temple of the universe. With this vision, Sri Ramakrishna's external worship stopped; there was no longer any need for it.

---

[1] 9. 26.

In the Bhagavad Gita, Sri Krishna mentions that the best kind of worship is that in which every moment and every act is offered to God. Walking, eating, speaking—all actions become an offering to the Lord. There is a famous verse in the Bhagavad Gita that says: "Brahman is the ritual, Brahman is the offering. Brahman is the one who offers to the fire that is Brahman. Those who see Brahman in every action will find Brahman."[2] All actions are given the color of worship. Whatever we do out of love is an offering to the Lord; every breath is for God; every moment is an offering to Him. Our entire life becomes an offering to the Divine.

Swami Vivekananda revived a distinctly spiritual form of worship: the worship of God in humanity. This is a very effective Vedanta practice for this age. We have to feel the presence of God in all men and women, but not as a mere idle contemplation. Just as love, in order to be dynamic, must manifest itself through action, so the worship of God in humanity must declare itself through concrete action, through service. Wherever there is need—physical, mental, or spiritual—there is the opportunity to serve humanity through tangible action. That is worship, Swami Vivekananda said, and he taught us how to perform this worship. We are to remind ourselves that it is the Atman, the universal Spirit residing in all beings, that we are worshipping. Let the giver kneel down and the receiver stand still and receive, for it is the same spirit of worship practiced in the temples; it is not a question of charity. It is God that we serve, not a particular person. Let the mother who is feeding the child think that she is worshipping God in the child. Let one who is nursing the sick, or teaching, consider it the worship of God. This attitude is a change of outlook. It is this new outlook that Swami Vivekananda, the modern prophet of Vedanta, wants us to practice; this is what he called "practical Vedanta."

When we turn to prayer, however, we are in the position of one who wants something from God. We stand before God as a helpless child, or a humble servant, asking for help. Though we

---

[2] 4. 24.

may not need God to provide us with food or shelter, yet other difficulties remain in the form of disease, death, and other numerous crises in our lives. Unable totally to dispense with the need for God, we pray to Him for help with our needs. Here again, as noted in the case of worship, our scriptures say that an initially selfish motive is better than a total rejection of God.

Of course, our prayers are not always effective. At such times, we should not lose faith in God, but remember that God is responsible for all phases of the cosmic process. What we call disease, death, and many other evils are also part of this process. If God does not listen to an individual prayer to save a particular life or to cure a particular disease, we should attempt to enlarge the scope of our vision to include the whole world process. What may appear to be an evil to me may not be so in the cosmic perspective. Even if God has not responded to a selfish prayer, the act of praying gradually prepares one for a purer type of prayer.

Prayer without any worldly motive is a powerful means for bringing about spiritual fulfillment. Praying to God for Self-knowledge, even for five minutes, connotes partial fulfillment, because the very process of praying purifies the mind, and gradually lifts it until temporary communion with God is attained. No wonder, then, that great illumined souls constantly pray: "O God, please grant me devotion, please give me faith." Such a prayer does not imply a lack of faith or love; the prayer itself brings its own fulfillment. Through all stages of purification, fulfillment runs parallel to the act of prayer.

The best type of prayer, Sri Ramakrishna said, is the prayer that asks for the highest things. In his characteristic way, he urged: "You shouldn't pray to God for eggplants and cucumbers. You should pray for Self-knowledge, discrimination, and renunciation." He himself continued to pray all his life in order to show the proper method of prayer. The highest prayer is to pray for great love of God. When that love is received, all other spiritual preparations, including tranquillity and control of the mind, spontaneously appear, and the true lover of God becomes illumined.

Why is prayer necessary? Perfected souls do not require any prayer, for they have attained Self-knowledge. Were we illumined souls, prayer would not be necessary for us. We, however, are still in the stage of aspirants who are surrounded by maya. We are bewildered and ignorant as to how maya makes its appearance, and how it affects our every thought and moment in our lives. Nor do we know how to get rid of maya; in fact, at any moment maya can overwhelm us. The mind may be tranquil and full of peace, compassion, and thoughts of God; again, the whole mental horizon can become covered with a cloud, and storms of desire or ignorance can overwhelm us. With our spiritual illumination thus obscured, we cannot cope with maya by ourselves.

Sri Ramakrishna offered prayer as the way to escape maya. He said, "Maya is nothing but the egotism of the embodied soul. This egotism has covered everything like a veil. God alone, the Creator of this world-bewitching maya, can save man from maya." Through self-surrender and resignation to God in prayer, Sri Ramakrishna demonstrated the way for us to slowly escape from maya. Great souls have attained illumination in this way, and they continued to practice prayer and humility the rest of their lives. Humility is absolutely necessary to keep the clouds of egotism from forming again.

As we analyze prayer, its twofold nature becomes apparent. We see the positive aspect of prayer when we pray for faith, purity, self-control, and devotion to God; we see its negative aspect when we pray to be separated from maya, or ignorance. Ignorance is opposed to spiritual knowledge, and so long as this ignorance exists, a loving God is required to help us conquer it.

It is by a combination of worship and prayer, based on love, that our minds become purified. We need both these practices to take us through the various stages of spiritual evolution until, ultimately merging, they give us the supreme object of our search—the vision of God.

MANTRA YOGA

MANTRA YOGA IS THE SPIRITUAL practice that unites the individual with God through the repetition of a mantra. A mantra is a holy name or word formula signifying God, with or without form and attribute.

The mantra can be just one word, a name of God like *Narayana. Namo Narayanaya*, "salutations to the Lord Narayana," is a two-word mantra. The three-word mantra, *Om namo Narayanaya,* is well known and is the traditional way for monks to greet one another.

Om is the most sacred word of the Vedas. It is considered to be one with Brahman—the highest Reality, personal or impersonal—and it is also the path to realize Brahman.

Those who follow the path of Advaita, the nondualistic approach to God, use mantras like *Om* or *Om Tat Sat.*

Om is the Logos, the undifferentiated word from which all the manifested universe has been created. "In the beginning was the Word, and the Word was with God, and the Word was God," we read in the Bible. "It is out of this holiest of all holy words, the mother of all names and forms, the eternal Om," Swami Vivekananda said,

> that the whole universe . . . [was] created. . . . These three letters . . . A. U. M., pronounced in combination as Om, may well be the generalized symbol of all possible sounds. The letter A is the least differentiated of all sounds. . . . Again, all articulate sounds are produced in the space within the mouth beginning with the root of the tongue and ending in the lips—the throat sound is A, and M is the last lip sound, and the U exactly represents the rolling forward of the impulse which begins at the root of the tongue till it ends in the lips. If properly pronounced, this Om will represent the whole phenomenon of sound-production, and no other word can

do this; . . . [Om] is indeed the first manifestation of
divine wisdom, this Om is truly symbolic of God. [1]

The Upanishads have revealed some short sentences called
mahavakyas, "great sayings," which are treated by those who
practice Advaita (nondualistic) Vedanta as mantras. Two of these
sayings are: *Aham Brahmasmi* (I am Brahman) and *Tat Tvam
Asi* (Thou art That).

Buddhism also prescribes mantras for spiritual seekers,
such as *Buddham saranam gacchami* (I take refuge in
Buddha); *Dharmam saranam gacchami* (I take refuge in
Dharma); *Sangham saranam gacchami* (I take refuge in the
Holy Order). These three sentences together form the three
vows of refuge, the repetition and contemplation of which
strengthen the spiritual life of the Buddhist seeker. In some tra-
ditions of Christianity and Islam the repetition of sacred sayings
and the divine name is also practiced.

In Hinduism, the use of the mantra during meditation on
God is widely prevalent. This practice comes from the central
belief proclaimed in the Vedas and other scriptures that the
nama—the name—is not different from the *nami*—the
named.

Brahman is described as the Supreme Sound—*Shabda-
Brahman*. It is from this concept of Shabda-Brahman that the
deep reverence for the holy name has sprung. The Taittiriya
Upanishad declares: "Om—this word is Brahman" and "Om is all
this."[2] This declaration is echoed in many of the sacred books
of India.

The first step of mantra yoga is to repeat the holy name
with great faith in its efficacy. The principle mentioned earlier
is that the mantra is one with the Ishta, the Chosen Ideal of
God, which may be a divine incarnation or the Supreme Self. In
the beginning, this is a difficult concept to understand. It will
be sufficient at the primary stage if the spiritual aspirant can

---

[1] *The Complete Works of Swami Vivekananda* (Calcutta: Advaita Ashrama,
1973), 3: 57-58.

[2] Taittiriya Upanishad 2. 7.

154 practice japa, repetition of the mantra, remembering that the mantra is connected with the power of divine consciousness. The aspirant should think that the holy name is creating spiritual vibrations in the body-mind-prana system. This vibration is not a material energy, such as magnetism, heat, or electricity, but spiritual energy.

Gradually, the spiritual seeker merges the mantra vibration into the movement of prana, the life-force. He or she begins to experience the unification of the two movements. This leads to the higher experience that the movement of prana itself is mantra repetition. The japa has been transferred from the tongue or throat to the life-force operating in the body. Every action of the prana becomes a vibration of the mantra.

As a result of this practice, a great harmony descends into the prana. What is achieved by the practice of pranayama in raja yoga, the yoga of concentration and meditation, is accomplished more completely in this stage of mantra yoga.

If the repetition of the mantra is directed to the five sense organs—eyes, ears, nostrils, tongue, skin—these organs become purified, and the corresponding five sense perceptions—sight, hearing, smell, taste, touch—become purified. We know that sense objects constantly draw the mind outward causing distractions, agitation, and suffering. When the sense organs become more imbued with sattva—purity and calmness—this state of things changes. Then whatever we experience through our senses will no longer agitate the mind. We read in the Gita, "One who is self-controlled moves among objects of lust and hatred, free from attraction and aversion. That person attains tranquillity."[3]

The tranquillity indicated by this verse can be attained by the practice of mantra yoga. In a way, practicing mantra yoga is more effective than attempting direct control over the senses. If love of God or Self-knowledge be the ultimate aim of life, then the purification of body and senses is essential. This purification is easily obtained by mantra yoga.

The organs of action can also be purified by the practice of mantra yoga. If japa is continued during such physical activities as moving the limbs, working, gardening, sweeping, etc., then

[3] Cf. Chap. I, section 3.

the corresponding organs of action undergo an inner transformation. The spiritual aspirant gradually begins to feel a spiritual vibration in the movement of the organs. In a song by the great eighteenth-century saint Ramprasad, we read:

> O my mind, you can worship Mother Kali in any way you please, as long as you repeat the mantra given by the guru day and night. Ramprasad declares with great delight that the Divine Mother is present in every activity. When you lie down, know that you are making obeisance to her. Meditate on Mother even while you are asleep. When you walk around the town, think that you are circumambulating the Divine Mother. All sounds that you hear are her mantras. . . . When you eat, think that you are offering an oblation to her.

The next step is to apply the mantra to the mental waves. Endless thoughts and emotions are constantly arising in the mind. It is indeed difficult to stop them. In the Bhagavad Gita, Arjuna mentions this problem to Sri Krishna, who replies, "Certainly, O Arjuna, the mind is restless and hard to control. But it can be subdued by constant practice and the exercise of detachment."[4]

The practice of mantra yoga in this context communicates the great power of the holy name with faith and love to the mental waves. In this practice there is not a bit of the toughness or aggressiveness that is required to challenge the mind directly. The distractions of the mind naturally become calm by the divine influence inherent in the mantra.

When the body, senses, prana, and mind become infused with sattva by the practice of japa, it is then time to purify all objects and phenomena outside ourselves. This is possible and should be done. The endless sky above, according to our normal vision, is material. But when you look at the sky, and connect it with the divine through the inner repetition of the mantra, the material space will change its appearance. The goal of the mantra, namely divine consciousness, will be peeping from the sky. The sky will appear to be a shawl on the cosmic

---

[4] 6. 35.

156 body of God. In a similar manner, the moon, the sun and stars above, the trees, flowers, streams, forests, hills, deserts, and living beings on earth or in water—all of these endless segments of the universe—can be purified by the mantra and be experienced as parts of the cosmic body of Satchidananda—Existence-Knowledge-Bliss absolute.

In the next stage of mantra yoga, the necessity of directing the mantra internally and to objects externally is transcended. The mantra is identical to the Ishta. This understanding should increase in strength as the mantra is repeated. The form of the Chosen Ideal or the impersonal idea of God should be present in the mind. As this practice ripens, the mantra and the Ishta, with or without form, become increasingly unified. *Mantra chaitanya*, that is, the divine consciousness implied in the mantra, will then be awakened. No more will there be doubts that the mantra is one with God. The heart will be filled with joy and peace.

Slowly it will be felt that the mantra as Shabda-Brahman, Sound-Brahman, is emanating from the innermost center of the universe; the meditator's heart has become, as it were, one with the heart of the universe. Not only that, but every object and event in the cosmos will be perceived and will be seen to function in the great Reality which is the mantra.

In this stage of mantra yoga, the word is increasingly revealed as Consciousness. The mantra is felt to be the radiant light of Consciousness. That light spreads out in the mind and prana, flooding the heart with immeasurable peace.

The devotee experiences the form of the Ishta as the light of Consciousness. The meditator's love for the Ishta becomes immensely intensified. For one who follows the path of jnana, knowledge, the mantra clearly reveals the deepest reality of the Self. Mantra chaitanya, the divine consciousness of the mantra, and *Atma chaitanya*, the divine consciousness of the Atman, become one.

When the mantra is transformed into Consciousness, the whole universe is experienced as Consciousness emerging from mantra consciousness. The five *bhutas*—the basic elements that comprise this universe, and all that is made of them—are then nothing but the emanation of Consciousness. The declarations of the Upanishads expressing Brahman or

Atman as pervading everything, such as, "All this verily is
Brahman" and "Atman alone is all this," become living to the
spiritual aspirant by means of mantra yoga.[5] At this point there
is no longer any repetition of the mantra in the usual sense of
the term. The mantra is no longer merely a word or words, but
one with Satchidananda, God as infinite Existence, Knowledge,
and Bliss.

The mantra, Shabda-Brahman, is continually revealing itself
in its own glory. The culmination of this glory can be said to be
the final stage. The body, mind, and prana are all expressions of
the mantra chaitanya; so is this vast universe.

Nothing else exists but the mantra as Consciousness—
Consciousness far away, Consciousness near, nearer, nearest. As
if one colossal flood had inundated everything, all names and
forms merge in one vast ocean of Consciousness. In this stage,
is it possible to perceive such dualities as great and small, gross
and fine, outside and inside, preceding and succeeding, and so
on? Only as long as the sublime experience of all-pervading
Consciousness has not come will we use terms associated with
space and time. In Consciousness there is neither space nor
time. Space and time spring from Consciousness. When
Consciousness is realized as the Supreme, both space and time
merge into Consciousness.

Can we describe this supreme glory of Shabda-Brahman in
words? No, we cannot. We read in the Taittiriya Upanishad:
"Whence words together with the mind turn away unable to
reach, that is the supreme bliss of Brahman. He who knows this
becomes free from all fear."[6]

Thus, at the ultimate level of Shabda-Brahman, words have
become wordless, forms have become formless, all multiplicity
has unified in Consciousness residing in that transcendent
glory beyond mind and speech. The seeker is mute, the mind
transcended.

By holding onto the mantra—the holy name received from
the spiritual teacher—with faith and love, experiencing the revelations of the mantra step by step, surely we can reach this
ultimate goal of our spiritual life as declared by Vedanta.

---

[5] Chandogya Upanishad 3. 14. 1 and 7. 25. 2.

[6] 2. 9.

THE SOUND
OF THE MANTRA

AFTER A SPIRITUAL ASPIRANT HAS received spiritual instructions and a mantra from a qualified teacher (which happens as a result of much good karma in the past), the aspirant has to repeat the mantra day after day with unfaltering faith, patience, and perseverance. Japa may be practiced with the fingers (as shown by the teacher) or with a rosary or mentally.

The scriptures and realized souls tell us that the mantra is the sound form of the Ishta, the Chosen Ideal of God. It is possible to experience the divine love and knowledge of the Ishta through the practice of japa. With unshakable faith and love for the mantra, the spiritual aspirant should practice repeating the mantra until the mantra becomes "awakened." God, who previously had seemed to be only a concept, will then appear to the aspirant as an indubitable truth. As the sages have declared, "Fulfillment is attained by japa. The goal is reached by japa. Realization comes from japa."

Sri Ramakrishna explained japa visually:

> Japa means silently repeating God's name in solitude. When you chant His name with single-minded devotion you can see God's form and realize Him. Suppose there is a piece of timber sunk in the water of the Ganges and fastened with a chain to the bank. You proceed link by link, holding to the chain, and you dive into the water and follow the chain. Finally you are able to reach the timber. In the same way by repeating God's name you become absorbed in Him and finally realize Him.[1]

---

[1] M, *The Gospel of Sri Ramakrishna*, trans. Swami Nikhilananda (New York: Ramakrishna-Vivekananda Center, 1952), pp. 878-79.

The experience of God comes to the aspirant either with form or without form. A devotee likes to think of the form of the Ishta during contemplation. Either before or during japa, he or she mentally places the Ishta in the lotus of the heart, directing the mind on that form. The mantra should be repeated simultaneously. The more a person is absorbed in japa, the more living the Ishta's form becomes.

The vision of the Ishta in the heart brings great peace and joy. Even if the vision occurs only once, the result is far-reaching, strengthening the devotee's faith and devotion. Such a vision transforms the character of the devotee, because he or she tangibly feels that the Ishta is always residing in the heart. This idea is never forgotten. All doubts about God end once and for all, and there is an increased manifestation of patience, forbearance, and love in the devotee's everyday life.

The spiritual aspirant who is drawn to the formless aspect of God meditates on the all-pervading Satchidananda, both externally and internally. Those aspirants who have a mantra of a personal form of God can also, if they wish, meditate on God's formless aspect. Sri Ramakrishna said that the divine is both with form and without form.

The forms of God are manifestations of the all-pervading Satchidananda. "In whatever way you approach Me, you shall have my grace," promises Sri Krishna in the Bhagavad Gita.[2] Sri Ramakrishna used to repeat, "Satchidananda Krishna, Satchidananda Shiva, Satchidananda mayi Ma." The implication is that Shiva, Krishna, Kali or any other divine form has as its foundation the formless Satchidananda. The aspirant who practices japa and meditates on the formless God can, by stages, have the direct experience of the Formless. In the beginning of our spiritual practice, we have to rely on either space or the ocean as symbols of Brahman. Just as on the material plane the ocean's endless waves appear and disappear, the aspirant can experience all segments of the universe as waves of Consciousness bubbling up on the formless Satchidananda.

___

[2] 4.11.

In the primary stage of spiritual practice, japa is experienced as a very low sound coming from the tongue and the throat. Similarly, in the primary stage, the aspirant considers himself or herself to be a devotee of God who repeats the holy name in order to experience love and faith and finally to have His vision.

Sometimes japa is done mechanically like a machine. The mind does not feel any sweetness. Questions arise: How can the mind be quieted by the repetition of mere sound? How can God be reached through the mantra? Our teachers tell us that this feeling of dryness and doubt is inevitable in the beginning, but one need not be afraid or depressed. One has to keep one's faith strong and, without thinking of the result, continue japa with steadiness. The preliminary distracted condition of the mind soon goes away.

As love for japa increases, the quality of the mantra's sound undergoes a change. The mantra then no longer comes from the tongue or throat, but is felt to be originating from the depths of the heart. Slowly the distinction between the Ishta's mantra and the Ishta's form melts away. Sound and form merge and become one.

As our faith that the Ishta is present in the mantra grows stronger, the presence of the Ishta and our love for Him or Her becomes deeper. Many spiritual aspirants have left hints of their experience of the mantra in songs and hymns. Ramprasad sang: "I have tied the divine name of Mother Tara in a tuft of hair on my head. I am ready to depart from this world, singing the name of Durga." For this type of aspirant, all worship, meditation, and prayer have taken their abode in the name of the Divine Mother. The name being tied in a tuft of hair on the head implies that the name is most intimately present in all three states of existence: waking, dreaming, and deep sleep—in fact, in any situation of life. For Ramprasad, the distinction between the Divine Mother and Her name has disappeared. The poet has no more doubt or fear. His heart remains forever unperturbed.

With continued practice, the sound of the mantra increasingly assumes subtler forms. Coming from the depths of the heart, the mantra begins to flow through the bloodstream, pervading the entire body. The heartbeat seems to become one with the sound of the mantra. The movement of the mantra goes to other areas, such as breathing, nerve action, and muscular activity. All these activities are expressions of spontaneous japa. Japa begins to be unceasingly repeated in every part of the body, and then japa becomes a total, unifying process which involves the whole physical body.

Next the mantra is communicated to our mental waves. Normally our minds express themselves in endless waves which make us laugh, cry, and restlessly rush about. There is no end to our thoughts, desires, reflections, and emotions. The faster these movements are, the more our minds are disturbed. For the mind's peace and harmony, we can try to control these mental waves in several ways.

One wonderful and certainly effective way to control the mental waves is to transmit the mantra to the mental waves. Just as the movements of our limbs can be felt to be the resounding of the mantra, the mental waves appear to the aspirant to be the resonance of the mantra. The dancing of the mind is an expression of the joy of the mantra. The whole mind has now joined in japa. When an aspirant who has attained this state sits for japa, the sound of the mantra seems to suffuse the entire body, mind, and prana. Even the ego reverberates as the sound of the mantra. As the result of this absorption in the mantra, an inexpressible peace is experienced. All the sense impressions from past lives are transformed into a sublime calmness.

From the standpoint of knowledge, distractions are also expressions of the one, immovable Consciousness. Thus, to see the vibration of the mantra in the movement of the mind is a spiritual experience of a high order.

We can experience the expansion of the mantra into the outside world. Innumerable sounds are constantly entering our ears—the murmuring of the wind, the thundering of lightening, the babbling of the brook, the rustling of leaves, the chirping of birds, the buzzing of flies, the humming of bees, the calls of different animals, the endless noise from human beings, the clatter of machines, and so on. Can all of these physical sounds be raised to the spiritual? A seemingly impossible task indeed!

Yet if we believe in the Sound-Brahman of the Upanishads, then this experience is attainable at the individual spiritual level. One of Ramprasad's songs says: "All that you hear are indeed mantras of the Divine Mother. The Mother's body is made from the fifty letters of the alphabet. Each letter generates a different name." Ramprasad's experience was that Mother Kali is revealed as words created from the alphabet's letters, so in every sound he heard the reverberation of Mother's name. No sound was able to distract his mind because sound itself had become his mantra. The world of sound is heard as a cosmic and spiritual reverberation of the aspirant's mantra.

Apart from sound, there are other perceptions in the external world—form, taste, smell, and touch. Can the mantra capture these sense impressions? The answer of the Upanishads is that any sense impression can certainly be experienced as an expression of the mantra. God and the name of God are one. When this conviction becomes unshakable, then all sense knowledge appears to be the sound of the mantra. The Chandogya Upanishad states: "Verily all this universe is Brahman."[3]

According to the Mandukya Upanishad, Om has four *matras*, or measures: the three letters A, U, M, and the fourth measure which is *amatra*, or silence. The fourth does not belong to the category of sound; it cannot be described or even thought about. Whatever is within the reach of our minds and bodies belongs to the first three matras. The symbol of the formless Brahman is amatra, the fourth expression of Om. In the formless Brahman there is no creation, preservation, or dissolution. There is no bondage or liberation. But when the formless Brahman comes down, as it were, to God with attributes, He becomes the God that is worshipped in the religions of the world, responsible for creation, preservation, and dissolution. He then becomes understandable to our minds. We can worship Him and we can pray to Him.

We can say that the formless Brahman's amatra brings out the three primary sounds, A, U, M—the first causal word, AUM

---

[3] 3. 14. 1.

(or Om). From Om all other words representing various objects spring forth. Every object in this universe has become associated with some name; we look upon the universe as one vast totality of objects and one totality of all sounds. From the spiritual outlook, the objects and their sound designations are the same. Every object has its sound counterpart, its name. When spiritual knowledge is revealed, the apparent difference between objects and their corresponding names disappears. It is possible for a spiritual aspirant to find that the mantra which comes out from the tongue, throat, or heart has pervaded every corner of the universe, internal and external.

The experience of the all-pervading mantra sound can also be called the experience of Shabda-Brahman, Sound-Brahman. Thus God, who is Sound-Brahman, gradually leads the aspirant from lesser truths to the one ultimate Truth. Sound-Brahman is eternal. The sound that is heard, reflected, and described is, in the subtle state, the inexpressible Sound-Brahman.

THE COMPANY OF GOD THROUGH THE HOLY NAME

TWO FRIENDS CAN ENJOY EACH other's company in many ways. They can sit and talk, go to a restaurant or movie together, or they may share mutual interests such as swimming or fishing. There is no limit to the ways in which they can enjoy each other's companionship, and each way is rewarding. They like to be together.

In a similar way, a serious devotee wants to feel the presence of God and commune with Him. The devotee's greatest desire and aim in life is to realize God. Yet the world with its many distractions blocks that communion. For although God is present everywhere—both within and without—maya, or ignorance, hides His face. Therefore, a devotee must practice being in the company of God in as many ways as possible.

Let us not think that the devotee alone seeks God, and that God does nothing. The teachers of bhakti yoga, the devotional path to God, tell us that God is even *more* eager to have the company of His devotee, for in this vast world there are very few who seek God for His sake alone. Millions of people seek God for some selfish or worldly end, but rare is the person who can say that he or she is seeking God, not for wealth or miracles, but simply because he or she loves God. In bhakti yoga, this type of seeker is called a first-class devotee. Such a devotee increasingly wants to feel the presence of God and to feel His presence in everything.

Devotees can have the company of God in numerous ways. They can go to a temple or holy place and meditate; they can read the holy scriptures and contemplate God, or they can sing devotional songs and worship with incense, flowers, and other rituals. In the Indian spiritual tradition, another way to have the company of God is through mantra yoga, the repetition of His holy name.

Mantra yoga is a wonderful way to bring oneself closer to God—even to the state of supreme unity, the apex of spiritual life. In the state of supreme unity, everything in the universe— space, time, mountains, rivers, stars, millions of living beings—is seen as the substance of God. Then we realize that it is God who continuously projects this vast phenomenon of life, and that this universe is not different from God.

The practice of mantra yoga has its roots in the basic philosophy of the Word; this philosophy states that the universe is formed from sound vibration, the different levels of vibration forming words.[1] Again that vibration, from another angle, is a vibration of the mind in a universe of ideas. Expressing these ideas are corresponding words, so that word vibrations and mind vibrations eventually merge into one Consciousness. It is Consciousness that appears as words, and it is Consciousness that appears as mind. Thus according to this philosophy, everything that a person experiences is the vibration of sounds. The ultimate Reality is God as sound, from which all other sound vibrations—as word and mind vibrations with their various concepts—come.

Through contemplation and meditation a stage can be reached where one's mind becomes totally fixed on Om as Shabda-Brahman, or Sound-Brahman. Sound vibration goes through the various strata of the mind deep into one's consciousness. All the mind's ideas slowly merge into Om, and eventually the subtlest sound merges into the soundless (ashabda) Brahman.

In the spiritual tradition of the Upanishads, the sound Om was originally the highest symbol of God, either personal or impersonal. Later, worship through other names of God such as

---

[1] Swami Shraddhananda is referring to the philosophy of Logos, which was given expression in the opening lines of St. John's gospel: "In the beginning was the Word, and the Word was with God, and the Word was God." Swami Vivekananda said in this connection, "Orthodox Hinduism makes *Shruti*, the sound, everything. The *thing* is but a feeble manifestation of the pre-existing and eternal idea. So the *name* of God is everything: God Himself is merely the objectification of that idea in the eternal mind." [*The Complete Works of Swami Vivekananda* (Calcutta: Advaita Ashrama, 1973), 8: 270.]—Ed.

Krishna, Shiva, Vishnu, and the Divine Mother developed, and these names were considered equal to Om. Thus, if one repeats any name of God with faith and understands that the name of God is really God Himself, one realizes that the holy name contains the totality of all experiences.

Our minds are normally diverted in many ways. We are constantly experiencing the multifarious instead of a unified existence, and so we cannot attain peace. Peace can come only when the mind becomes still. Mantra yoga declares that any name of God, practiced with faith, concentrates the mind and leads us to increasingly subtler phases of the mantra vibration and eventually to the experience of supreme unity.

The holy name is like a tiny seed which, when planted, slowly sprouts and finally grows into a gigantic tree. While apparently simple, it contains great potential; just as God is simple, yet the storehouse of infinite power. Whatever we value in life—power, beauty, love, greatness, compassion—is in God because He is the totality of all our values. In the same way, a person who practices mantra yoga has faith that God's name is the repository of all God's attributes. One's faith may be weak at first, but with practice, faith grows. One increasingly feels that the holy name is bringing about a spiritual transformation.

In the beginning a devotee practices the mantra mentally or sometimes, when alone, audibly. The devotee sits quietly with great love, because the holy name is a great treasure. Just as when a beloved son or daughter has departed, and the mother remembers the child's name with deep feeling, so God's name has the power to invoke love. As the devotee repeats the mantra, he or she feels the purification that comes with the holy name, and as a result, the mind becomes increasingly peaceful and collected. When this stage is reached, several things must be added to one's spiritual practice.

First of all, the devotee must consciously direct the mantra to the different elements of body and mind. Take for instance the prana, functioning in the body as the life energy that sustains the heart, breathing, nervous system, and all the processes that keep us alive. The spiritual aspirant does not want the body, mind, and prana to remain as they previously were; if they remain tools of ignorance, they will impede our spiritual progress at every step. At every point our senses are stumbling blocks, because the plan of nature is not to release us from ignorance but to keep us bound. That is God's play. We are in reality divine, and the soul is ever infinite and free; but maya causes us to forget our divinity. The prana, which generally keeps the body alive just for procreation and enjoyment of the senses, must be purified and made divine. Similarly, we must purify our eyes, ears, hands, and all parts of the body, as well as the mind in its various states. Then the body will become a real temple. All desires and passions related to the various senses will cease. This can be achieved by directing the mantra, knowing that the holy name is God's power. That power is the greatest purifier; if it touches any spot, that spot becomes holy.

The first thing that we notice when directing the mantra to the prana is that the breathing and heartbeat become slow. All the vital processes inside the body become calm. Similarly, when we direct the mantra to different parts of the body, those parts also become still. If the eyes are restless, they will become calm by directing the holy name to them. In this way, one by one, the mantra can be directed to every part of the body and vital processes in order to bring the whole system under control.

Finally, the mantra must be applied to the restless, wandering mind, which is constantly producing irrational desires, emotions, and conflicts. The mind will try to run away; it will be afraid of this purifying process. Just as when we want to kill weeds with chemicals, certain weeds helplessly succumb but others defy the attempt, so the mind will protest. The mind will say, "You purify the prana, the eyes, and everything else, but let me be." Yet the power and peace of God lie within the holy name which quiets the mind. In this way, the actual repetition of the mantra goes very deep; it occurs not only in the mouth, but it also goes to the deepest core of one's personality, to one's consciousness. One should remember that repetition of the mantra is God's company, because the mantra is God. As one's faith intensifies, it will be increasingly felt that God is always present in the mind, intellect, and ego. Then one enjoys the company of God more and more, and the body and mind become ready to have increasingly subtler experiences of God-consciousness.

At that stage, all the elements to which the mantra was directed no longer act as obstacles, but rather come to the aid of the devotee. They participate in mantra yoga. The prana will say, "You need not direct your mantra to me. I will help you with the mantra myself." All the vital processes—breathing, blood circulation, and so on—will then be felt to be repeating the mantra. Of course, such repetition will not make the usual sound; it will be a subtle vibration. The devotee will feel that wherever the prana carries out its functions, the mantra is being repeated—not in human sound, but as a subtle spiritual vibration. He or she will also feel the vibration in the eyes. Whenever the eyes see something, the devotee will feel that the mantra is being repeated by them; he or she will feel that the perception which comes to the eyes is a vibration of the mantra. When the ears hear sound, it will appear to be part of one's japa. When the hands move to touch something, the devotee will feel that they are repeating the mantra. All sense perceptions together with the various parts of one's psychophysical system will vibrate with the mantra as they participate in the devotee's mantra yoga.

When that experience comes, the calmness and peace that descend on one's mind and heart are really wonderful. There is no longer any struggle. The mind is no longer being forced to do japa—it voluntarily comes to one's aid and repeats the mantra. The company of God through the mantra becomes all-pervasive.

Finally, the devotee becomes convinced that the holy name of God is really God himself, the source of everything. He or she increasingly feels that the universe has become the mantra. The mantra as God, as the Divine in the form of the Word—the ultimate vibration—takes over and absorbs everything. The devotee feels that the whole universe, all thought and experience, is the vibration of the mantra. The diversity and manifoldness of the universe begin to disappear.

The universe at different stages has different types of vibrations—light is one kind of vibration, heat is another type, and the mind is another. But on the spiritual level, the aspirant knows that all these diverse vibrations are ultimately spiritual vibrations. For the aspirant, they are vibrations of the mantra.

When this stage is reached, the devotee feels that everything within and without is the mantra; then the repetition of the mantra ceases. The mantra merges into silence. When we study Om, we see that it consists of three sounds, namely, A-U-M; there is also a fourth element, which is called amatra, which means silence. Likewise, in the divine name there is an audible part which becomes increasingly subtle as it goes deep into our consciousness; eventually it merges into silence. This is what we call samadhi. In this state we go beyond all concepts and, as the Upanishads say, "beyond the reach of mind and words." The highest truth cannot be expressed. There is no longer any repetition of the mantra, either gross or subtle.

Thus, when supreme God-consciousness comes, the play of maya is over, and one is not regretful. Yet in some cases, the devotee's mind comes down again and sees the world—but not as before. The company of God as the mantra is with him or her. The devotee acts, meets with friends, and lives in the world; but God, as the vibration of the holy word, is always present. The mantra comes not only from the eyes, ears, body, and actions, but from the surroundings as well. Thus, when one returns to the normal plane of consciousness, it is a different life, a wonderful, illumined life, free from fear, delusion, and ignorance.

PERVASION
OF THE MANTRA

THE MANTRA IS ONE WITH God; there is no difference between God and His name. This belief, though initially weak, gathers strength as the spiritual seeker continues to practice japa. In the beginning, the taste for the practice may not be very strong. It seems to be a sort of mechanical enterprise. But if the spiritual seeker does not give up and continues to repeat the mantra as instructed by the teacher, the mantra eventually becomes "awakened." It removes the evil tendencies of the mind, gradually filling it with pure joy and the consciousness of God. The light of the mantra begins to illumine the heart, which is slowly raised to higher levels of spiritual reality. One such level can be called the pervasion of the mantra.

Those who have received initiation (received a mantra) from an illumined teacher keep the mantra in their hearts as a precious, sacred treasure. Those who have been initiated should not be asked by curious friends and family members about the mantra they have received. It is an entirely private matter. During meditation the mantra should be brought out from the treasure house of the heart. The seeker should continue to repeat the mantra almost inaudibly or silently, with as much faith and love as possible. If japa is continued with patience, it is sure to reveal the truth of God. The expression *japat siddhih*, perfection through japa, is well-known among spiritual seekers.

The scriptures and the teachings of illumined souls tell us that in order for the mantra to be raised to the level of enlightening power, three things are essential: purity of body and mind, eagerness for the vision of God, and detachment from sense-pleasures. Sri Ramakrishna said about the mantra:

Yes, there is no doubt about the sanctity of God's name. But can a mere name achieve anything, without the yearning love of the devotee behind it? One should feel great restlessness of soul for the vision of God. Suppose a man repeats the name of God mechanically, while his mind is absorbed in "woman and gold." Can he achieve anything?[1]

One attains God through japa. By repeating the name of God secretly and in solitude one receives divine grace. Then comes His vision.[2]

Why, is the name of God a trifling thing? God is not different from His name. Satyabhama tried to balance Krishna with gold and precious stones, but could not do it. Then Rukmini put a tulsi-leaf with the name of Krishna on the scales. That balanced the Lord.[3]

We say that God is Satchidananda, Existence-Knowledge-Bliss absolute. Whatever exists—whatever comes to our knowledge, and whatever is joyful—inheres in God. God is Sat because there is no break in His existence. He is Chit because there is no limit to His knowledge. He is Ananda because all that is dear and lovable has its source in His bliss. Spiritual seekers who practice japa should think of the mantra as Satchidananda; during japa they desire that their limited existence enter into the unlimited existence of Shabda-Brahman, Brahman as sound, and that their hearts may be filled with the blissful, spiritual light of the mantra. Of course this desire cannot be fulfilled in one day. Spiritual disciplines have to be practiced with patience, hope, and faith. Eventually the time will come when the mantra becomes fully awakened.

---

[1] M, *The Gospel of Sri Ramakrishna*, trans. Swami Nikhilananda (New York: Ramakrishna-Vivekananda Center, 1952), p. 190. Sri Ramakrishna used the expression *kamini-kancana*, which literally means "woman and gold," to denote lust and greed. When speaking to women devotees, Sri Ramakrishna spoke of "men and gold."—Ed.

[2] Ibid., p. 588.

[3] Ibid., p. 386.

172

The awakened mantra cannot be kept concealed in the throat or in the heart. The mantra begins to expand. When there is a flood, the waters of the river overflow the banks and spread far and wide. In the same manner, the awakened mantra emerges not merely from the lips or tongue or throat, but from all directions and all things.

Expansion of the mantra involves the spiritual transformation of every object that is touched by the mantra. Here are some examples: Through our physical eyes we see numerous objects. Let the mantra be directed to the eyes. Wherever the eyes now turn, the glow of the Spirit radiates from the object seen. The visual experience then will seem to be the sound of the mantra. Whatever visual knowledge comes through the eyes is now equivalent to the repetition of the mantra. When japa was done audibly or mentally, the mantra was nothing but a subtle sound. Now that "sound" has been transformed into "form." The aspirant sees the patterns that are floating in the mind as the expression of the mantra. Mantra consciousness is thus extended to all forms seen by the eyes. By the touch of the mantra the physical ears become transformed into "divine ears." Whatever sounds enter the ears are not ordinary sounds. They are the vibrations of the mantra.

Similarly the three other sense-organs—those of touch, smell, and taste—become companions of the mantra when enlivened with mantra consciousness. Every experience of touch, smell, and taste brings the joy and satisfaction of japa. In the same way, any other part of the body besides the sense organs can also be spiritualized by the expansion of the mantra. The heartbeat, breathing process, blood circulation, the flow of nerve currents—all these can be experienced as the play of the mantra. The mantra manifests in every segment of the body. Within one word, all the vital activities of the body participate in japa.

The mind, memory, discriminative faculty, and ego do not remain idle. They also participate in the spiritual aspirant's japa. To the aspirant, whatever waves arise in the mind represent the mantra; any definite ascertainment by the *buddhi*, the discriminative faculty, appears to be the revelation of the mantra. The ego gives up its assertion of individuality and becomes a spiritualized expression of the mantra.[4]

The pervasion of the body, mind, and prana by the mantra is not a small blessing. Sri Ramakrishna used to say that the body of a devotee is the playground of Consciousness. When the aspirant practices japa with faith, love, and patience, his or her psychophysical system becomes a "divine body." Heaven, as it were, descends into that body. The Kena Upanishad points this out: "One who realizes the existence of Brahman behind every activity—whether sensation, perception, or thought—that person alone gains immortality."[5]

If it is true that the mantra received from the teacher is verily Shabda-Brahman—Sound-Brahman—then it is but natural that its expansion will continue even outside the body-mind complex. The Upanishads say that Brahman is all-pervading. In a similar manner, spiritual aspirants who perform japa want to experience the mantra as all-pervading. This is one positive step toward Self-knowledge. The aspirant directs the mantra toward the sky and says, "O sky, you are Consciousness revealed to me; be one with my mantra. I want to hear the unstruck *anahata* sound of the mantra in your vast reality."[6] Similarly, when the mantra is experienced in the air, the aspirant experiences the divine dance of the mantra in the gentle breeze, in the strong wind, and in the terrible storm.

By deep contemplation, the other three elements—energy, water, and earth—are similarly transformed into the mantra. Any kind of energy considered from the spiritual perspective is understood to be the unfoldment of the mantra. We encounter water in many different forms such as rain, mist, clouds, ice,

---

[4] According to classical Hindu texts, the mind is composed of the *manas*, which receives sense impressions; the *chitta,* or memory; the *buddhi*, the discriminative faculty, which discriminates between "this" and "not this" and decides upon a course of action; and the *ahamkara*, the ego, which claims sense impressions for itself and establishes them as individual knowledge.—Ed.

[5] 2. 4.

[6] The *anahata shabda* literally means the "unstruck sound" which may be heard in higher states of meditation; the sound is Om.—Ed.

174 waterfalls, rivers, and oceans. The spiritual seeker tries to feel all these water forms as the mantra.

The green fields, trees, and also the deserts, hills, and mountains are all various forms of the earth. However soft or hard, however small or large, into each of these forms the mantra has the power to enter. The spiritual seeker experiences all these forms as merging into one unified, homogeneous Consciousness.

The Upanishads and the Bhagavad Gita have described the all-pervasiveness and all-inclusiveness of the Supreme Spirit. There is not a single object or event in which the consciousness of the Supreme Self is absent. If the mantra is Sound-Brahman, if the name is one with the One possessing the name, then the mantra also is all-extensive and all-embracing.

By the grace of God and the spiritual teacher, fortunate spiritual aspirants during the practice of japa can feel the pervasion of the mantra from time to time. Let us remember a passage from the Mandukya Upanishad:

> "Om" is indeed all this. All that is past, present, and future is indeed Om. And whatsoever transcends past, present, and future, that also is Om.[7]

These are not empty words. The illumined sages of the past as well as many spiritual seekers of later times have realized the truth of this statement. If we continue to practice japa with love and patience, the mantra will soon become "awakened" and it will pervade the body, mind, and prana, as well as everyday action; it will flood the world around us.

Our spiritual lives will then become blessed to the utmost.

---

[7] 1. 1.

CONTEMPLATION WITH OM

THE UPANISHADS PRESCRIBE MEDITATION ON *pranava,* the word-symbol Om. In Vedic days the sacrificial fire would be started by rubbing two pieces of wood together. The Svetasvatara Upanishad uses this process to illustrate a technique for meditating with Om.[1] The body of the meditator is to be considered the lower piece of wood and pranava, the upper one. Repetition of Om with faith and reflection on its meaning is likened to rubbing together the two pieces of wood. This repetition raises the mind to subtler and subtler levels of consciousness until it gradually comprehends the indwelling pure Consciousness—our own true Self. Self-knowledge is the fire kindled by the friction of the wood.

According to the Upanishads, all sounds spring from the ultimate primal sound—pranava, or Om. Om pervades all possible sounds and words. Brahman is the totality of all existence; anything that exists is in Brahman. Since any segment of existence can be symbolized by a word, the totality of existence can be represented by Om, the origin and support of all words. Om is regarded as the word-symbol of Brahman. While repeating Om the meditator should think that the Self hidden in the body is like the latent energy of heat in the wood. By the practice of repeating Om, the fire of Self-knowledge is ignited.

During the process of this meditation, the mind goes from the gross to the subtle until eventually everything merges in Om. No longer will the horn of a car disturb us as the noise of a car; it will be Om. Even the tremendous noise of a jet plane merges into Om. Whatever thought arises in the mind will at once disappear into Om. All experience will become Om. The

---

[1] 1. 12. 13.

176 mind will be perfectly calm. There will be only Om, the anahata (unstruck) primal spiritual vibration. Finally, that vibration also merges into the indescribable silence of the Self. By the repetition of Om, the pure Consciousness that is latent in every part of the body and mind emerges as a tangible experience. Our true Self is the other name for Brahman, the Supreme Reality.

This particular technique of meditation is analogous to Pascal's law of hydrostatics: When pressure is applied to a body of water in an enclosed vessel, that pressure will exert an equal force in all directions. Using this analogy, during japa we should think that the holy sound Om is reverberating through every fiber, every cell of the body; it is exerting its force on every nerve, every muscle, every organ, every breath.

Direct the word-symbol Om to every thought and every emotion, and those thoughts and emotions will become purified. The meditator should remember that this great mantra, Om, is a spiritual power that transforms every part of the body and mind. All thoughts become divine thoughts. All experience is transformed into divine experience. Such is the effect of this meditation. Eventually the Self—now hidden—becomes manifest, and that manifestation is the fire of knowledge.

An equally powerful meditation is described in the Mundaka Upanishad. Here the imagery concerns shooting at a target with a bow and arrow. In meditation visualize Om as a bow, and your mind as an arrow. Just as an archer fixes the arrow in the bow and aims at the target, in meditation place your mind in the bow of the Om and aim the mind at the target, Brahman. Meditation is the act of shooting. The mind is aimed by the repetition of Om. As a result one-pointedness is achieved. The one-pointed mind meditates on Brahman as pure Consciousness. Through meditation the mind becomes unified with pure Consciousness which is revealed as the meditator's true Self.

In ancient India there were many different uses of Om in daily life. These practices gave a spiritual value to all actions. Some of these uses are found in the Taittiriya Upanishad.[2]

---

[2] 1. 8.

Sometimes Om was used to communicate approval; it meant, "I have understood."

One should feel that every action is an offering to the Divine, every action is spiritual. If one is eating, one should say, "Om, let me eat." Before opening a book, one can say, "Om, let me begin the study." If we introduce Om into our secular activities, the mind becomes pure and holy.

The Mandukya Upanishad divides the sound of Om into four matras, or constituents—A, U, M, and amatra, or the silent portion. The first three represent the three states of waking, dreaming, and deep sleep, respectively. The amatra stands for the seer of the three states; namely, the Self. The Self can never be designated by a word because words relate to objective reality. The amatra indicates the eternal Subject. The Taittiriya Upanishad declares: "When a Vedic teacher wishes to obtain Brahman he utters Om; thus desiring Brahman, he verily obtains Brahman."[3]

The Upanishad reminds the student that Om is Brahman, the highest Reality, and Om is all that exists. This is a matter of experience, and this experience does not come all at once. First this solid external reality has to be seen as ideas, and then all ideas have to be seen as words. Later, all words merge into Om. When this experience is attained, the aspirant realizes that everything comes from the ultimate sound, Om.

---

[3] Ibid.

PLACING
THE MANTRA

MANTRA NYASA, THE PLACING OF a mantra, is an important part of ritualistic worship. *Nyasa* means placing special short formulas—"seed" words (*bija* mantras)—on different areas of the body by a movement of the fingers or palm. The idea behind this is that the places once touched become mystically enlivened. A well-known maxim declares that in order to worship the divine, one must first become divine. As a first step toward becoming divine, the worshipper tries to purify the body and infuse spiritual power into his or her limbs at the beginning of the ritualistic worship through various nyasas. Apart from ritualistic worship, some people practice nyasa in order to bring about harmony in the body and mind. The effect of nyasa in this case is similar to that of pranayama, or breath control.

Practices like breath control and nyasa belong to the domain of *vaidhi bhakti*, that is, preparatory devotion, and are governed by the regulations of religious dogma. But when deep love for God springs in the heart, these ritualistic practices cease to be important. Bhakti then reaches the level of *raga bhakti*, a passionate attachment to the Divine. Shankara says in one of his devotional hymns:

> I know neither charity nor meditation. I am ignorant
> of Tantra, hymns, or mantras. Neither am I familiar
> with puja and nyasa yoga. O Mother, Thou art my
> only refuge.[1]

However, the concept of placing the mantra can be used in meditation in various ways. Those who follow the paths of devotion and knowledge can make use of its spiritual value and

---

[1] *Bhavanyastakam.*

thereby gain deeper and subtler levels of experience. A spiritual seeker who has received a mantra from a qualified teacher should have great faith that the holy name of God is one with God. Spiritual reality is condensed in the mantra. The mantra is Shabda-Brahman, Sound-Brahman. The scriptures declare that when the mantra is practiced with great intensity, love, and faith, it becomes awakened and opens up amazing vistas of spiritual knowledge.

The Yoga scriptures speak of six spiritual centers in the body. Sri Ramakrishna pointed out that the heart is an excellent place for meditation. One can apply mantra nyasa by visualizing a beautiful, full-blooming lotus in the region of the heart. This is the seat of the Ishta, the Chosen Ideal of God. While repeating the mantra, the aspirant should first think that the mantra is purifying the seat of the Ishta and making it radiant. The Chandogya Upanishad states that the student should seek and ask about the inner abode:

> Within the city of Brahman, which is the body, there is the heart, and within the heart, there is an abode. It has the shape of a lotus, and within it dwells that which is to be sought after, inquired about, and realized.[2]

The next nyasa is on the image of the Chosen Ideal in the lotus of the heart. The aspirant visualizes the form of the Ishta shining in the light of Consciousness while simultaneously directing the mantra toward the Ishta; these twin mental activities are then gradually merged into one. The sound of the mantra then becomes one with the form of the Ishta. Both are eternal Consciousness—*Paramatman*, the Supreme Soul. The experience of hearing the mantra and seeing the Ishta is unified in Consciousness. The state of mind in which these two different experiences become one is called *prajna*, or pure comprehension. Says the Katha Upanishad: "The Self is realized only through prajna."[3] And again, "That Self, hidden in all beings, does not shine forth; but it is seen through one-pointed and subtle intellects."[4]

---

[2] 8. 1. 1.
[3] 1. 2. 24.
[4] Ibid., 1. 3. 12.

As the practice of the mantra progresses, the Ishta transcends form and merges into the formless Satchidananda; the mantra also goes from sound to the Soundless, to Shabda-Brahman. The Mandukya Upanishad speaks of the four components of the supreme sound Om. The first three components of Om—A, U, and M—are *vyakta,* or expressible. The final part is *avyakta,* or inexpressible; it is described as amatra, without a part. What is true of Om also applies to other mantras. The Ishta mantra, placed on the Chosen Ideal during contemplation, leads first to the vivid living presence of the personal aspect of God, and then finally merges into the soundless Brahman.

Sometimes spiritual seekers practice contemplation with open eyes. In that case the external altar containing the Ishta's image or picture becomes the spiritual aspirant's heart. The mantra, which is repeated in the mind and directed to the external image of one's Chosen Ideal, then becomes "enlivened" with Consciousness. In the course of spiritual practice, the aspirant will feel that there is no difference between the Ishta's external image and the sound of the mantra; the aspirant will find that the sound of the mantra itself is seated on the altar as the Ishta's image.

According to the Vedanta scriptures, prana is divided into five components and is responsible for the body's biological functions. Respiration, circulation, digestion, and nerve reactions, along with the various movements of the limbs and mental activities, are all animated by the power of prana. Sri Krishna says in the Bhagavad Gita: "Abiding in the bodies of all living beings, I consume many foods, turning them into the strength that upholds the body."[5]

Consciousness is superior to prana. The Supreme Self is indeed pure Consciousness; the power of prana really comes from the Atman. In the Brihadaranyaka Upanishad we read: "Those who have known the Prana of the prana, the Eye of the eye, the Ear of the ear, and the Mind of the mind, have realized the ancient, primordial Brahman."[6]

---

[5] 15. 14.

[6] 4. 4. 18.

In the stage of ignorance we do not know that the functions of prana are ruled by Consciousness. If mantra nyasa is practiced on the prana, its biological nature slowly becomes purified. The individual's prana becomes transformed into divine prana.

While repeating the mantra, the mind should be directed toward breathing, heartbeat, circulation, and other functions. Gradually the meditator will feel that the prana's movements are really vibrations of the mantra. What was previously a biological pulsation is now experienced by the spiritual seeker as a pulsation of mantra consciousness, or spiritual consciousness. The repetition of the mantra has spread throughout the activities of the prana. The aspirant is not only repeating the mantra with the throat or tongue or mind, the mantra is being spontaneously repeated wherever there is any movement of prana. The prana, thus "purified" by mantra nyasa, gradually leads to higher experiences of Consciousness.

The Katha Upanishad states: "The Self-existent Creator made the senses turn outward. Accordingly human beings look toward what is without and see not the inner Self."[7] If mantra nyasa is practiced on the functions of the senses, their outgoing tendencies will be considerably arrested. When the eyes experience any visual form, let that experience be connected with the power of the mantra. Then visual knowledge will be transformed into divine knowledge. If the mantra is directed to a sound impression received through the ears, the sound will cease to distract the mind. The spiritual aspirant's sight and hearing will glow with the light of Consciousness. In a similar way, other sense experiences can be spiritually transformed. This pervasion and deepening of the repetition of the mantra brings a beautiful peace to the heart.

Body consciousness is a terrible obstruction to our spiritual life. This burden can be lightened through mantra nyasa. Instead of constantly attaching the "I" concept to the gross body, let the mantra be "placed" all over the body. The biological body will then be a spiritual entity. Ramprasad sang: "The name of Mother

---

[7] 2. 1. 1.

Kali is the heavenly wish-fulfilling tree that I have planted in my heart. I have sold my body in the marketplace of the world and bought in exchange the name of Mother Durga." Here "sold my body" means to be freed from body consciousness. The holy name of the Divine Mother has now taken its place.

It is difficult to meditate deeply on our Chosen Ideal because of the mind's incessant wanderings; various methods have been prescribed to aid concentration. Mantra nyasa is an excellent aid. If mental waves engage in the repetition of the mantra, and thus establish a spiritual friendship with it, the mental waves will no longer behave as enemies. "The uncontrolled mind behaves as a foe to oneself," says the Bhagavad Gita.[8] If the mantra is directed to a mental wave, it becomes illumined with the light of Consciousness and then becomes a spiritual companion.

The Svetasvatara Upanishad describes the relative world as *brahmachakra*, the wheel of Brahman: "On this wheel the individual self revolves endlessly."[9] This brahmachakra is in truth Brahman Itself, but because of ignorance the individual soul does not realize this; he or she sees the One as multifarious, and experiences the universe as constantly changing. The individual soul thus becomes overwhelmed by the dualities of pleasure and pain, hope and frustration, life and death. If we could understand the brahmachakra to be Brahman and feel the presence of the immutable Divine in the manifold world, our confusion and helpless rotation on the wheel of birth and death would end, and we would attain supreme peace.

Just as by mantra nyasa we can spiritualize the body, prana, senses, and mental functions by raising them from their material level to that of the Spirit, harmony of the Spirit can be brought into the diverse segments of the world of our experience.

Let the mantra be "placed" on the vast sky, the ocean, rivers, forests, mountains, trees, plants, and meadows. Let the mantra be fixed on human beings, animals, traffic noise, and on any

---

[8] 6. 6.
[9] 1. 6.

other segment of the universe that comes to our experience. 183
The mantra as Sound-Brahman will transform that material segment into spiritual radiance.

Thus, knowing the name of God to be God Himself, we can
apply the power of the mantra inside and outside of us and
bring our experience of existence to the sublime unity of
Satchidananda. So long as the mantra is with us, God is with us;
wherever the mantra is placed, the Divine is revealed there.

MANTRA BINDU

MANTRAS ARE NOT ARBITRARY COMPOSITIONS, but rather words imbued with spiritual power, revealed in the hearts of the seers of God, or *rishis*. The principal use of a mantra is spiritual. When the mantra is received from an experienced teacher and repeated for a long time with faith and love, it creates miracles in spiritual life. Japa purifies the heart's blemishes, purifies our unwelcome desires and passions, and opens the door to higher spiritual experiences.

There are, however, those who seek mantra initiation for secular reasons. They believe in God and seek His grace in times of worldly need. So in any important affair, good or bad, like the birth of a child, marriage, starting a business, or recovery from a serious illness, they pray to God for His blessings or relief. Sometimes help comes, sometimes not. Yet such secular application of a mantra should not be condemned, because association with God on any level of life is beneficial, unless the motive is selfish or unethical.

An earnest spiritual seeker, however, repeats the mantra only for a spiritual purpose; namely, a direct experience of God. This experience can come in many ways.

In bhakti yoga the devotee tangibly feels the presence of God in the heart. Sometimes he or she may have a clear, living vision of the Ishta. Through japa, ritualistic worship, prayer or other devotional practices, the devotee develops increasingly intense love for God. The different objects of love are transformed into one great Divine Love which completely changes the pattern of his or her thinking, emotions, and actions. The devotee feels that the material world is thoroughly imbued with the love and power of God.

The devotee establishes a human relationship with God. God is father or mother, master, friend, or even sweetheart, and the devotee is the child, servant, friend, or lover. These human relations, working on the spiritual plane, bring indescribable joy, sweetness, and strength to the devotee. Whatever action the devotee performs, he or she does not claim to be its agent. God is the doer, the prime mover in his or her life.

In jnana yoga the goal is to experience one's true Self—the Atman—which is one with God's transcendent Reality. This Reality is infinite Consciousness and Bliss. The jnana yogi's path is the path of vichara, analysis. In this world's transient flux, the jnani wants to find that which is unchanging. Examining the contradictions of life, the jnani rejects as non-Self whatever is self-contradictory. Our true Self is imprisoned, as it were, in the cage of the body, prana, and sense enjoyment.

In the jnana yoga process of analysis, six basic disciplines are mentioned in the Vedanta scriptures: *sama*, control of the mind; *dama*, control of the senses; *titiksha*, forbearance; *shraddha*, faith in the words of the scriptures and the guru; *uparati*, inwardness; and *samadhana*, meditation. Within the depths of our being is the eternal, unborn, and undecaying Self, untouched by ignorance. This is the Reality behind the phenomenal world.

The identity of the individual self, the *jivatman*, with the Supreme Self, the Paramatman, is declared in many passages of the Upanishads: *Aham Brahmasmi*, I am Brahman; *Tat Tvam Asi*, Thou art That; *Ayam Atma Brahma*, This Self is Brahman. The repetition of the mantra slowly lifts the mind from the phenomenal world to the comprehension of this identity. For the jnani, the phenomenal world is an illusory creation of the mind, like a dream. By the steady practice of the repetition of the mantra, the mind becomes withdrawn from the manifold and rests in the true Self. This is the beginning of Self-knowledge.

The words Brahman and Atman are interchangeable. Both point to the unborn, timeless Reality, which is the basis of all knowledge. *Sarvam khalvidam Brahma*: "All that we perceive is Brahman," asserts the Chandogya Upanishad; "All this is the Atman," says the Brihadaranyaka Upanishad.

The mind has to be trained to see every object of experience as Consciousness. The Kena Upanishad states: "Brahman is really known when It is known in each state of consciousness; thereby one attains immortality."[1]

The spiritual aspirant's mantra, which is Sound-Brahman, can take the role of both God with form as well as God without form. During a subtle state of japa, the spiritual seeker can feel that all creation is issuing forth from the mantra. The vast universe, every part of it, is a projection of the mantra as Sound-Brahman. And, conversely, any objective knowledge, great or small, can be merged into Sound-Brahman. This may also be called *laya yoga*, the "yoga of dissolution." To the spiritual aspirant, the universe is no longer vast. The mantra is absorbing it, bit by bit. From God with form, the Ishta mantra moves toward the Formless. But it does not change its dimensions by absorbing the universe. It is aptly described in the famous peace chant from the Vedas: "Filled with Brahman are the things we see, filled with Brahman are the things we see not. From out of Brahman flows all that is, from Brahman all, yet is He still the same."

We may say that the mantra, after absorbing the universe within itself, remains as a *bindu*, a point. A point has no dimensions. It is neither big nor small, neither far nor near. The mantra, however, is not a geometrical point. It is Supreme Consciousness as the minutest, nonmeasurable, inexpressible totality. The experience of the mantra bindu is hinted at in the Chandogya Upanishad: "From the dark [nonduality] I attain to the variegated; from the variegated I attain to the dark. Shaking off evil as a horse shakes off dust from its coat . . . I, having fulfilled all ends, obtain the world of Brahman."[2]

Gaudapada, in his commentary on the *Mandukya Karika,* describes the grand experience of the mantra bindu in this way: "One who has known Om, which is without sound and is of infinite sounds, and which is ever peaceful because of the negation of duality, is the real sage, and none else."[3] What Gaudapada calls Om is equally applicable to any mantra.

---

[1] 2. 4.

[2] 8. 13. 1.

[3] 1. 29.

Sri Ramakrishna in his teaching of the harmony of all yogas indicates the great majesty of the mantra bindu. Divine love eventually leads to the totality of all loves converging in an immeasurable point. Ultimately, all karma is experienced as proceeding from the source of all movement. All yogic disciplines eventually lead to the final concentration on the *Antaratman*, the inner Self, which is nothing but the mantra bindu.

ROSARY FOR JAPA

THOSE WHO PRACTICE JAPA—THE repetition of the holy name—often use some kind of rosary, a string of beads (*mala*) made from different sorts of material, such as rudraksha seeds, tulasi, sandalwood, or crystal. The rosary hangs on the middle finger of the right hand and the beads are turned by the thumb toward the devotee as the mantra is repeated. Primarily the rosary facilitates the counting of the mantra. Its second function is to help the seeker concentrate. The restless mind is bound to have a certain amount of concentration in the process of using the rosary. The psychological intent of using a rosary is to direct whatever attention the mind can muster to the repetition of the mantra, letting the rest of the mind wander as it pleases. But, besides these two uses, there is another function of the rosary, which is to lift the mind to higher spiritual levels.

How the rosary contributes to spiritual life cannot be understood in the very beginning. As our faith and love for the mantra grows in intensity, this function of the rosary begins to be understood. Then the spiritual seeker uses the rosary, but not for the sake of counting or for concentrating the mind. The rotation of the rosary becomes a part of the power and joy of japa. To the spiritual aspirant, it seems that the whole world is participating in the rotation of the rosary. The various experiences of the five senses—sound, touch, taste, sight, and smell—can no longer distract the mind. They have entered into the rosary as friends, seeking closeness to the Divine. Each bead is now a segment of the world of sense experience.

If during the practice of japa the rosary can help to minimize the distractions of the mind, it is certainly a great friend in our spiritual adventure. When we begin to understand this function of the rosary, then the technique of japa begins to change. The material that constitutes the rosary also changes, no longer being confined to tulasi, rudraksha or crystal.

The prana that ceaselessly functions in the body through inhalation and exhalation—as if forming a circle—can well be substituted for the rosary. The prana then becomes a spiritual companion over and above its biological function. The meditator experiences the mantra being repeated in harmony with the rotation of the breath. The mantra consciousness united with the movement of the breath transforms the biological prana into divine prana. The biological prana maintains, protects, and strengthens the organs, blood vessels, and millions of cells. The role of the divine prana is to communicate spiritual power to the blood stream and cellular systems. The prana as a rosary does not keep count of the number of times the mantra has been repeated. But, being animated by the consciousness of the mantra, it brings under control the biological passions of the body, such as lust and anger, and gives them a spiritual direction. Japa with the rosary of the prana does not preclude the use of our own rosary beads. Just as a symphony is enriched by various instruments playing together, japa with the prana rosary brings a new value and depth to the normal use of the rosary.

The mind can also be a rosary for japa. The rise and fall of the mental waves—our thoughts—form the circular movement of the rosary. Our mental waves are then no longer distractions but rather spiritual associates in the practice of japa. The sound of the holy name from the throat or heart touches the mental waves and purifies them, raising them from the level of rajas and tamas to that of sattva. The spiritual seeker may at first feel discouraged when the waves of the mind disturb the practice of japa. The distracted mind is viewed as an enemy, but this practice removes that problem. The mind has now become a rosary for japa, the different mental waves being the beads of the rosary. Each mental modification is illumined by the light of the mantra. The mind is no longer an enemy, but a companion of japa. The mental waves are no longer engrossed in maya; they have become radiant by the reality of pure Consciousness.

We find a discussion of "true desire" and "false desire" in the Chandogya Upanishad. As long as the basic Reality—Existence-Knowledge-Bliss absolute—which holds and permeates everything, has not been known, all objects of desire are "covered with falsehood."[1]

On the other hand, for that blessed person who has realized the Paramatman, the infinite Consciousness in the heart, "false desires" are transformed into "true desires." The Chandogya Upanishad further applies this experience to food, fragrance, music, and even to erotic objects. These objects at one time deluded the mind as objects of gross enjoyment, but now they glow as radiations of the infinite Consciousness, the Paramatman. The same objects of "false desires," thus transformed into being one with the Eternal, become "true desires." Just as the mythical philosopher's stone converts base metal into gold, any object of sense enjoyment conjoined with the light of Consciousness becomes a piece of Satchidananda. When the mind is meditated upon as a rosary for japa, the mental waves, illumined by Consciousness, become part of the spiritual Reality.

Our physical body can be a rosary for japa, our various limbs being comparable to the beads of the rosary. The mantra is repeated in the throat or in the mind and the subtle vibration of the mantra resonates throughout the parts of the body. These components of the body have now joined in the aspirant's japa. The head no longer wants to nod or droop. The eyes, ears, nose, hands, and feet have now given up their wanderings. A circle has been formed from the upper to the lower and from the lower to the upper parts of the body. Every segment of this circle receives the touch of Consciousness. The aspirant distinctly feels that his or her body is no longer a biological unit but filled with Consciousness through and through. The Katha Upanishad says:

> This body is a city of eleven gates belonging to the
> eternal Atman whose consciousness forever shines.

---

[1] 8. 1-3.

One who meditates on the Ruler of that city knows
no more sorrow. Attaining liberation, the illumined
soul is forever freed from birth and death.[2]

For an aspirant immersed in the practice of japa, the mantra
as Sound-Brahman becomes that Ruler. The body is where that
Being plays. When the king is in residence in the city, all houses
and gates and roads and passages maintain order and tidiness.
In a similar way, when the mantra becomes established within,
all the organs and other parts of the seeker's body glow with
the light of the great mantra.

This universe can also become a rosary for japa. The sun is
one bead, the moon another, the constellation of stars yet
another. The sky, the ocean, forests, deserts, and mountains are
the other beads. Whatever parts of the universe come to the
mind become beads of this cosmic rosary. The mantra consciousness, after extending beyond the prana, mind, and body,
has pervaded infinite space and time. The entire cosmos has
been linked with the consciousness of the mantra. As a consequence, all creation has given up its material mask and has
revealed its spiritual nature.

This experience is hinted at in a well-known verse in the
Katha Upanishad which may be paraphrased as follows: The
same Brahman-consciousness which, lodged in our hearts, illumines body, mind, and prana, now radiates far and near in all
objects and phenomena—in fact, through all of nature. As the
sun He radiates heat and light. He is the glory of the heavenly
spheres and He pervades all space. Brahman appears on the
earth as fire; He is in all human beings and in all deities; He is in
the sky and the birds that fly in the sky; in aquatic creatures, in
vegetation, and in the endless chain of living beings on earth.
He is shining as the white snow on mountain peaks. He directs
all changes in the universe and yet His true nature is unchanging. He is the True and the Great.[3]

"Om is Brahman," the Vedas have declared. Om is God with
form and also God without form—the Paramatman, beyond

---

[2] 2. 2. 1.

[3] 2. 2. 2.

192 speech and mind, beyond all causality. The Hindu scriptures have combined various names of God with this primary word, Om. Thus various mantras, pertaining to various manifestations of God and suitable for a variety of seekers, have come into existence. The primary assertion of the Vedas has not been abandoned in the diversity of mantras.

Our ideas of God—both formless and with form—become living truths with the help of the mantra. The rosary is especially helpful in the practice of japa. As the mantra's spiritual revelations increase, the rosary also undergoes a spiritual transformation. This transfiguration slowly and gradually fills the physical body, prana, mind, and the whole of the material universe with Consciousness. Eventually, japa of the mantra dissolves into that infinite supreme Unity: soundless, intangible, formless, undecaying, tasteless, eternal, odorless, having neither beginning nor end.[4]

The rosary of beads vanishes into that indescribable nonduality.

---

[4] Ibid., 1. 3. 15.

THE OCEAN
AND THE WAVES:
MEDITATION ON THE ABSOLUTE

IN VEDANTA SCRIPTURES, THE OCEAN and the waves have
been extensively used as a metaphor to convey the idea of
Brahman, the highest truth of God. In fact, the Brihadaranyaka
Upanishad refers to Brahman as the ocean, *samudra*. [1]

Brahman is not a material entity like the ocean, but if we
use the ocean as a symbol, our minds will be better able to
understand Brahman as infinite Consciousness. Even though
the ocean is a limited form and therefore a limited concept, it
can effectively help us transcend all other limiting forms and
concepts, enabling us to realize the truth which is ultimately
beyond both space and time.

Sri Ramakrishna's first experience of God was as the infinite ocean of Consciousness. He began his spiritual life by worshipping and meditating upon the personal God—God as the
Divine Mother Kali. Through constant prayer and meditation
his desire for spiritual experience became so keen and intense
that he was finally granted the vision of God by the Mother—
but not as a particular, personal form of God. Instead, he had
the experience of the infinite, impersonal ocean of
Consciousness and Bliss, the ocean of Satchidananda. He felt
that waves of Consciousness, like waves in the ocean, were
everywhere, rushing toward him and enveloping him. The
entire material universe had been transformed into waves of
Consciousness which were dancing upon an infinite ocean of
Consciousness. Mountainous waves, like those of a storm-tossed
sea, were surrounding him, only with this difference: the ocean
was not a material ocean. The walls of the shrine where he worshipped, the image of Mother Kali, the articles of worship

---

[1] 1. 1. 2.

before him, and even his own body had all become waves of Consciousness.

Such an experience encompasses the sense of space, time, and individuality; then one experiences the ultimate Unity. One no longer feels that there is an ocean of Consciousness and its waves. The mind then goes to the Inexpressible. And this was Sri Ramakrishna's experience. In the beginning, he had felt that everything had become waves of Consciousness—the walls, the image, the articles, and his own body—but then he transcended even this experience, merging into what in Vedanta literature has been described as "neti, neti," not this, not this.

This ultimate experience is beyond mind, beyond speech, beyond all individuality. But this ultimate experience should not be confused with the state of dreamless sleep in which there is also no sense of time. There is a vast difference between the two. When we wake from dreamless sleep, the world is the same old world and we are the same old people, except that our bodies and nerves are relaxed and refreshed. Our personalities have not been transformed, and no new knowledge has come to us. The same old world of multiplicity remains.

On the other hand, when we have experienced everything as being waves of an infinite ocean of Consciousness, and when that experience also at last stops and merges into the inexpressible, indescribable Absolute, then when we return to a normal state of consciousness, we awaken with a new knowledge. We feel that everything has been transformed; everything that was previously experienced as multiplicity is really only Consciousness. Then at all times we know in our heart of hearts that everything is that infinite Existence, Consciousness, and Bliss; everything is really God. That experience of supreme unity transforms us and adds a new dimension to our lives. We become seers of God.

If we sit by the ocean's shore in a philosophical state of mind and watch the waves' delightful play, we can experience a very wonderful train of ideas. We can easily observe how each wave appears to be different from every other wave, and how each wave appears to be different from the ocean. By continuing to analyze and reflect, we can see that the waves and the ocean are made of the same substance. The waves are not really different from the ocean. The difference is only apparent, based upon the temporary appearance of the wave state. The real truth of the wave is that it is the ocean.

If we become a little creative while viewing the waves, we can imagine that two waves which are side by side have personalities and are friends. One wave is wiser. That wave has knowledge of Vedanta—it is a Vedanta wave! The other friend, however, is an ignorant wave. It has forgotten that the ocean is its home, its source of power, life, and joy. As the waves rise together the ignorant wave exclaims, "I am a forty-foot wave! I look like a mountain. See how beautiful and powerful I am!" But as they rise, the Vedanta wave only smiles. Finally, when they both begin to fall, the ignorant wave becomes afraid and begins to cry, "I am becoming smaller and smaller! I am disappearing!" Then the Vedanta wave very calmly says, "How foolish you are. Nothing has happened to you. Your real nature is one with the ocean. You are always in and of the ocean. You *are* the ocean. A temporary form came, and you have become proud of your power and glory, but you are always one with the infinite power of the ocean. We are simply merging into that infinite power of the ocean where there is no death. We are returning to our real nature. So why should you be afraid?"

In the same manner, a person who seeks the truth of the impersonal aspect of God should first train his or her mind by analyzing the external, material universe; then the aspirant should proceed inwardly to merge with the infinite Truth. These two practices have been elaborated in detail in the Upanishads to enhance and guide our meditations.

When we begin an external analysis, we find that anything that happens, happens in space and time. This vast universe is guided by natural laws, and each natural law obeys strict laws of causation. Similarly, our bodies and minds are a part of this vast, cosmic show which operates according to physical and psychological laws.

The sages of the Upanishads, however, discovered that our experience of the material universe is only a partial

196 experience. If we probe more deeply into the nature of this material universe, we find that there are finer and subtler levels of reality behind this gross manifestation. Today even scientists are engaged in this search as they explore the beginnings of creation. As they try to discover a first cause, their minds become involved in the problems of cosmology because this search for a first cause is natural and important for the human mind. It is not a luxury. It is the search for unity, a unity without which we cannot function.

If, for example, a man lives the life of a lonely vagabond—sometimes sleeping in roadside sheds, sometimes in open fields in a sleeping bag—such a person is really miserable. Why? Because the sense of unity with others is essential for human growth. There must be some kind of connection with others, a feeling of love and unity. If the same man acquires a family, a home, a job, and possessions, he naturally becomes happier. He will say, "Well, the whole universe may be alien to me. The sun may not belong to me. That garden may not belong to me. But at least I have this much." This identification with a part of his environment makes him happier; it makes him feel greater than just a small, isolated unit of existence. There is an inherent tendency in us to expand our personalities, to search outside ourselves for unity—unity not only with human beings, but also with plants, animals, rivers, and mountains as well. Therefore the sages of the Upanishads say that if we are seeking the highest truth of God, we will first have to expand our personality. We must not remain satisfied with experience as it naturally comes to us, such experiences are only a small phase of reality.

If we remain satisfied with just this material universe, we will not be able to grow spiritually. We may be very successful scientists, scholars, or businessmen, but the problems of life will not be solved. We will not be able to attain the peace, knowledge, and joy that resolve all doubts, and give us fearlessness and freedom. To seek the higher truth, we cannot merely accept what comes through the senses. Instead, we have to develop the powers and capabilities of the mind. Through spiritual practice, concentration, and meditation, our minds can experience increasingly profound intuitions; we can discover ever more subtle levels of reality. Then this manifold universe with its endless varieties of sight, sound, smell, taste, and touch will resolve itself into subtler shades of unity.

According to the Vedanta scriptures, the entire universe, including the mind, is composed of five elements which are the cause of all things. The first and most subtle of these five elements is *akasha,* or space. By a slow process of evolution, air comes from this fundamental akasha. From air, energy evolves; from energy, water comes; and then finally from water, matter in the solid state comes. We should remember, however, that these are all symbolic expressions of actual spiritual experiences. In other words, at one stage the mind perceives this universe as solid and material, but later, as the mind develops, matter is forgotten, and the universe appears to be made only of energy. In this way, through objective analysis, we can experience increasingly subtler levels of reality.

The sages say that Consciousness is the basis of akasha, or space. Consciousness is beyond both space and time; it is beyond all our normal experiences. The space-time continuum is not final. Beyond space-time is the vast, impersonal reality of God as Satchidananda—infinite Existence, Consciousness, and Bliss. And these three, according to Vedanta, are one.

Existence can never be isolated from consciousness. Whatever we think, feel, or see, is enveloped by knowledge. Whether we are seeing or experiencing a tree, a wall, our own body, thoughts, or emotions, we can know for certain that just as these are pieces of existence, they are also pieces of knowledge, or consciousness. At the same time, any experience is also bound to bring a sense of joy. For example, if we are shut in a dark, soundproof room for thirty-six hours, we will be miserable. Why? Because we miss the joy of seeing and hearing. But as soon as we come out of that room into the light, anything that we perceive—whether it be a cat, a dog, a tree, or even something that we do not like—that object will be, for the moment, a thing of joy for us. Therefore, if we continue to probe deeply, we will find that everything has three faces; namely, existence, consciousness, and joy. Every experience is a part of Satchidananda.

Again the analogy and imagery of the ocean is very helpful. For just as millions of waves arise from the ocean but really have their basis *in* the ocean, so also everything in this vast universe can be thought of as arising out of the ocean of Satchidananda. Everything has its source in Satchidananda.

Holding to this idea, we should imagine during meditation that any idea, thought, or emotion that arises is really a wave of Satchidananda. With this knowledge of unity, even unpleasant or terrible thoughts can be conquered by resolving them into the ocean-like totality of God—God as the infinite, impersonal Satchidananda.

In our normal, everyday life, we experience existence in a piecemeal fashion, always perceiving differences and dualities. But that is ignorance. If we are trying to realize the impersonal aspect of God, then we have to practice this meditation: Just as millions of waves are really the ocean, so also all experiences are waves of Satchidananda; they are part of Satchidananda.

If we practice this meditation, a time will come when all duality will disappear; the waves and the ocean will become one. But just as it happened to Sri Ramakrishna, the mind can rise still higher. We will be able to reach that state which cannot be described by thought or words: God as He is, God the indescribable Absolute. In other words, all the manifold stages of reality—space-time, matter, energy—will be resolved into the ultimate Unity, the self-existent, eternal truth of God.

When we are ignorant, we isolate ourselves from this great truth. We become petty, proud, and miserable. Seeing only the manifold, we become afraid. But when we understand that we are one with Satchidananda, that we exist in the infinite ocean of Brahman, we become proud of our real glory. We become fearless. We know that even though our little individualities—our bodies, our accomplishments, our possessions—may vanish like waves at any moment, we are nevertheless one with the infinite ocean of God.

The analogy of the ocean and the waves is very significant and helpful, because it takes us to the point from which we can make the ultimate journey into unity. Everything becomes one. Everything becomes Brahman, the ocean of Satchidananda.

When we become stabilized in this experience, we will be prepared for the final experience: that the infinite ocean, or Brahman, is not outside us, but rather inside as the Atman, as our own Self. Each of us then may rightfully claim: "I am that vast ocean of Satchidananda." At this point our spiritual practice takes the form of the meditation on the Atman, the emphasis being directed toward our own true nature.

Just as we analyzed and comprehended the external universe through increasingly subtle stages, so also we can analyze and comprehend ourselves through successively inward stages—as body, prana, mind, further and further, until we find that we are that infinite Ocean.

The ocean of Satchidananda is not in time and space. It is Itself: self-evident Reality, my soul, my Atman, me. And this vast universe is just a wave. The sun is a wave. The moon is a wave. The solar system is a wave. My body and millions of other bodies are just waves. Anything that is heard, seen, felt, or thought, is a projection of the Atman. Just as any wave is a projection of the ocean, so any experience is a projection of the Self. And I am that Self, that infinite ocean of Satchidananda. *Aham Brahmasmi*: "I am Brahman," as the sage of the Upanishads declares.

Through this meditation upon the subjective Truth, the Atman within, our minds eventually will reach the same state that can be reached through the analysis and comprehension of the external universe. Just as we objectively realize that "everything is Brahman," so we subjectively realize that "everything is me." We go beyond speech. Then we become speechless. We no longer say, "I am Satchidananda" but "What I am, I am." That is the highest knowledge of freedom.

Through the analogy of the ocean and the waves, practiced either objectively or subjectively, we arrive at the same goal—the inexpressible, indescribable Absolute.

SPIRITUAL
∾ GUIDANCE ∾

INSTRUCTIONS TO A DISCIPLE

The following letter was given as spiritual instruction to one of Swami Shraddhananda's disciples. These instructions, he wrote, "may be helpful in your practical sadhana."[1]

Impersonal meditation can . . . be practiced on Saguna Brahman.[2] Here Brahman has "gunas" or attributes or qualities—He is the Creator, Supporter, and Destroyer of the universe. He is our Master, Father, Grandfather, Mother, Friend, and so on.

There is no end to God's attributes. Remember that verse of the Shiva Mahimna Stotra: "If the earth be the paper sheet, the Ocean the ink pot, Sumeru Mountain the pen of Mother Saraswati [who] herself goes on writing through infinite time, still she will not be able to exhaust narrating your glories, O Lord Shiva."

The meditator can choose some attributes which appeal to him and meditate on Saguna Brahman.

Then Saguna Brahman can also be meditated on with forms—like Shiva, Vishnu, Kali, Lakshmi, etc.—also as avataras—like Rama, Krishna, Christ. Impersonal meditation on Saguna Brahman becomes personal when you use such attributes as Father, Mother, etc. Because then *you* the meditator have established a personal relationship with God. I will write a chart now regarding meditation:

---

[1] *Sadhana* is the practice of spiritual disciplines or austerity.—Ed.

[2] *Saguna Brahman* is the personal aspect of God; literally, "Brahman with attributes."—Ed.

204

MEDITATION

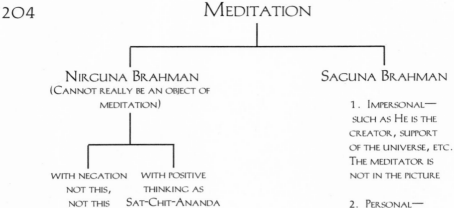

NIRGUNA BRAHMAN
(CANNOT REALLY BE AN OBJECT OF
MEDITATION)

WITH NEGATION
NOT THIS,
NOT THIS

WITH POSITIVE
THINKING AS
SAT-CHIT-ANANDA
(HERE THERE IS
NO PERSONAL
RELATIONSHIP)
SAT-CHIT-ANANDA
ARE NOT GUNAS OR
ATTRIBUTES OF BRAHMAN
THEY INDICATE THE
"SVARUPA" (NATURE)
OF BRAHMAN

SAGUNA BRAHMAN

1. IMPERSONAL—
SUCH AS HE IS THE
CREATOR, SUPPORT
OF THE UNIVERSE, ETC.
THE MEDITATOR IS
NOT IN THE PICTURE

2. PERSONAL—
WITHOUT FORM
(AS IN CHRISTIANITY,
ISLAM &
ALSO HINDUISM)

3. PERSONAL—
WITH FORM

4. PERSONAL—
AS AVATAR
WHEN YOU
ARE MEDITATING ON
SAGUNA BRAHMAN
YOU HAVE TO THINK
OF HIS GUNAS—
ATTRIBUTES, GLORIES

Nirguna Brahman cannot be an object of our direct meditation.[3] [Only] when the mind stops, Nirguna Brahman—the
Absolute beyond speech and mind—*(avang manaso gocharan)* reveals itself.

Nirguna Brahman is identical with man's True Self. Yet
there can and must be some practice of contemplation for
the approximate understanding of Nirguna Brahman. This
contemplation is really a form of negation. But there is also a
positive way.

Brahman is not space, is not time, is not matter, is not mind,
is not prana, and so on. The continued process of negation
eventually stills the mind and the reality of Brahman reveals
itself. Approximate positive meditation of Nirguna Brahman is
to think of Brahman as Satchidananda: infinite Existence, infinite Consciousness, infinite Ananda.[4] We have [the] experience
of "existence" all the time. Now Brahman is undivided, infinite
Existence—Sat. Similarly, we have experience of Consciousness
or Knowledge all the time. We are conscious of this and that.
But these are "pieces," fragments of Consciousness. Brahman, on
the other hand, is infinite Unbroken Consciousness. All
Consciousness of our practical life is coming from that infinite
Consciousness—Brahman.

Then Ananda or joy is also our well-known experience.
Broken pieces of joy are coming to us at different times and
occasions. Eating ice cream, watching an interesting T. V. show,
sipping coffee with snacks and so on. But Brahman is infinite
joy or blessedness. Now Existence, Consciousness, and Joy are
not attributes of Brahman. They are not really three different
things. Sat-Chit-Ananda form a Unity. It is called the "nature"
(*svarupa*) of Brahman—so far as we can objectively think
about Brahman.

Repeated meditation on Brahman as Satchidananda prepares the mind for the ultimate experience. The mind steps
away and the *avang manaso gocharan*—the Absolute beyond
mind and speech—shows its indescribably sweet face and then
also we understand that Nirguna Brahman is me—me—me—
my true Self.

---

[3] *Nirguna Brahman* is Brahman without attributes, the unconditioned
Absolute.—Ed.

[4] Pure bliss, unalloyed joy.—Ed.

EXCERPTS FROM
LETTERS TO A DEVOTEE

The following extracts were taken from Swami Shraddhananda's letters to a devotee.

❦

Giving spiritual transformation to desires can be done either by bhakti or by jnana. First one has to grow intense love for the holy name (mantra) and feel that the name and Deity are one. The form blends into Name and Name blends into form. Any distraction that comes to the mind is transformed by the mantra as a vibration or glow of the Divine. The distractions will be finally ashamed. Even if they come, they will be ignored. Before the emperor (the Ishta) what insignificant petty chief will dare to make noise?

So go on doing japa with great faith and love.

❦

[Your] guru's blessings are always with you. He brought you to Thakur and Ma and will never stop helping you.[5]

The sacred mantra received from the guru is one with [the] Ishta. This is realized slowly through years of sadhana. The mantra is like a vacuum cleaner. It sucks all the dark *samskaras* of the mind.[6] As the faith in and love for the mantra intensify, japa becomes extremely interesting. The ideas in my mantra articles are glimpses of these experiences.

---

[5] "Thakur and Ma" refer to Sri Ramakrishna and Sri Sarada Devi.—Ed.

[6] *Samskaras* are tendencies inherited from previous births that create a person's propensities in this life.—Ed.

So, child, go on with japa with love and faith. The distractions of the mind will be transformed into divine vibrations by the power of the mantra. Have patience.

⋙

Don't be alarmed if black marks come from the ink pot. At once throw your mantra on them.[7]

⋙

Every spiritual seeker has to be careful about *moha*, infatuation. Innocent love and reverence can turn to sattvic attachment. Only towards the Ishta and guru and highly spiritual persons "passionate" bhakti does not bind. It purifies the mind of the aspirant. Mantra japa and prayer are great antidotes to moha as they are to *kama* (lust) and *krodha*, (anger).

⋙

P.S.   Spray the mind for bugs with the mantra
Vacuum clean the mind's dirt from all
   corners with the mantra
Paint the mind with the mantra.

---

[7] The ink pot refers to the problem of cleaning an ink pot that is firmly situated on a desk. Since the ink pot can't be picked up, clean water has to be poured into the pot while the ink and dirt bubble up to the surface. The mantra has an analogous effect upon the mind. —Ed.

Excerpts from
Informal Talks

The following excerpts were taken from Swami Shraddhananda's informal talks with the nuns of Sarada Convent, Santa Barbara.

"We always live according to our liking. If I don't like to sit like this, I sit like that. That liking is an aspect of infinite joy. God is Infinite Joy. Even poison gives joy to some. We are surrounded by Infinite Joy.

"We have to apply this truth in all stages of our life. One can spiritualize even drinking a cup of tea." Reciting a verse from the Bhagavad Gita, he said, "*Brahmarpanam Brahma Havir*... Brahman is the ritual ... all is Brahman."

"Why does God do this, why does He do that? No human laws apply to Him. He is beyond causation. When everything goes nicely we say: 'How great You are!' When He apparently does not listen we say: 'Why did You do that?'

"Our happiness and misery are governed by the law of karma. Right actions bring good karma. Wrong actions bring bad karma. Sri Ramakrishna said that God is the Supreme Master. We do not understand, therefore we should not try to question why He does this or that.

"Sometimes we complicate our relationship with God by our self-interest. Pray for devotion! God listens and answers that prayer. Don't go for secular things; then the law of karma enters.

"When a crisis comes, a devotee can't help but pray for relief. Or the devotee says, 'Swami, can't you pray a little for my child?' We have to say yes.

"When I am confronted by a problem, I pray, 'Please help that devotee.' Then I add, 'You are the embodiment of all gods and goddesses. Please listen to my prayer as Ganesha [the Remover of Obstacles].'"

Swami Shraddhananda mentioned three ways of dealing with pain.

The first is to look upon pain as an expression of Consciousness. When asked whether he was using the word "consciousness" as equated with Brahman, he answered, "Of course." He said that everything is Consciousness.

Swami Shraddhananda said that this is not to deny pain. Rather, it is seeing pain as Shabda-Brahman, a vibration of Brahman. It is seeing pain in its real nature. When we know that pain is Consciousness, it stops. Everything is a projection of the Self, the Supreme Self. When we really experience this, we are free.

Someone with spiritual comprehension, he continued, can direct the mind in meditation to the pain and feel that the pain is Consciousness. It is all one. Then the pain leaves.

The second method of dealing with pain is the one used by Swami Turiyananda [a direct disciple of Sri Ramakrishna] during his carbuncle operation. By that method one withdraws the mind from the pain and puts it elsewhere.

Finally, a devotee will look upon pain as God's will: "The Lord is my Beloved."

The attitude one takes depends upon one's temperament and the degree of one's comprehension.

In describing *arati*, the waving of lights during the vesper service, Swami Shraddhananda mentioned a meditation in which the devotees are seen as small candle flames around Sri Ramakrishna. The devotees and Sri Ramakrishna merge and become one. "Bring the idea of oneness whenever and wherever you can," he said. "That is the message of the Upanishads. That is Vedanta."

As an example, he said that when the convent members sing the arati songs in the temple, they should "think that there

210 is one voice singing." They should use creative imagination to bring the idea of oneness in every action. This is how to try and practice Advaita Vedanta.

❧

"Every time you have an obstacle, cover the obstacle with the mantra. The obstacle will hang its head in shame.

"Sometimes it is not fun to do japa. It is boring. Never mind! Go on! If you do japa the way your teacher has taught you, it will open up a vastness.

"You can tap into the minds of all the great teachers when making japa." Mentioning the names of several direct disciples of Sri Ramakrishna, he continued, "Their bodies are gone, but their minds are living.

"When your own japa is not going well, you can draw on the japa of everyone in the temple. You can go to the Hollywood Center and draw on their japa. You can go to Sarada Math in India: 150 nuns are there. Or go to Belur Math: 1200 monks are there who make japa. Draw on the japa of the devotees.

"You have to continue the japa. You have to maintain sincerity."

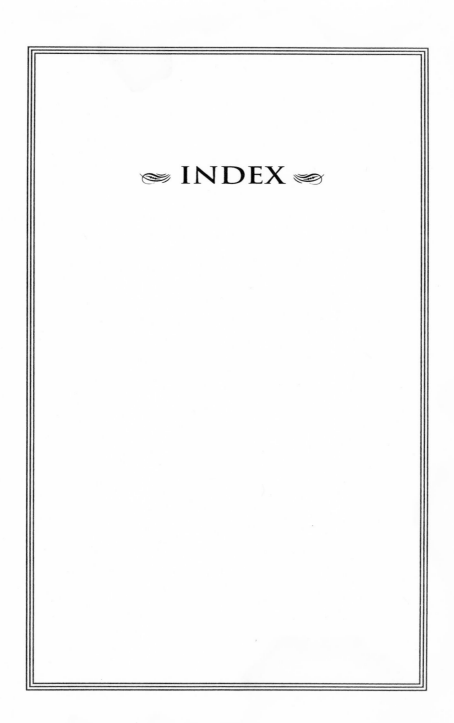

~ INDEX ~